WONDERFUL WORLD OF KNOWLEDGE

YEAR BOOK 1979

Disney's

Wonderful World of Knowledge

YEAR BOOK 1979

THE DANBURY PRESS

THE DANBURY PRESS

a division of Grolier Enterprises, Inc.

ROBERT B. CLARKE   *Publisher*

ISBN 0-7172-8123-X
The Library of Congress Catalog Card Number: 78-66149

Text on pages 34-37, 58-61, 78-81, 104-107,
and all Disney character illustrations
Copyright © 1979, Walt Disney Productions

COPYRIGHT © 1979 BY  Grolier
INCORPORATED
DANBURY, CONNECTICUT

Copyright © in Canada 1979 BY GROLIER LIMITED

PRINTED IN THE UNITED STATES OF AMERICA

CONTENTS

1978 AT A GLANCE

JANUARY 11. Two Soviet cosmonauts docked their Soyuz spacecraft to the Salyut 6 space station. They joined two other cosmonauts who had docked with the station in late 1977. This was the first time that two spacecraft had docked with a space station at the same time. It was an important step toward setting up a permanent space station. It showed that the Soviet Union could change crews and supply the station with food.

JANUARY 24. Cosmos 954, an unmanned Soviet spy satellite, re-entered the Earth's atmosphere and broke up. Parts of the satellite fell in a remote area in Canada's Northwest Territories. Canadian and U.S. scientists found some radioactive pieces of the satellite and its nuclear reactor. But it is believed that no people were harmed by the accident.

MARCH 17. The supertanker *Amoco Cadiz* ran aground and broke in two off the coast of France. Its cargo—some 200,000 tons of crude oil—leaked into the sea. This was the worst oil spill in history.

APRIL 6. President Jimmy Carter signed into law a bill that will allow most U.S. workers to work until they are 70 years old instead of 65. The law becomes effective January 1, 1979.

APRIL 18. The U.S. Senate approved a treaty that will give Panama complete control of the Panama Canal by the year 2000. A month earlier, the Senate had approved a treaty guaranteeing the neutrality of the canal.

APRIL 30. Japanese explorer Naomi Uemura became the first person to reach the North Pole alone by dog sled. His trip across the frozen Arctic Ocean covered 600 miles (965 kilometers) and took 54 days.

MAY 12. The U.S. Department of Commerce announced that hurricanes would be given both male and female names. For example, the second Pacific hurricane of 1978 would be named Hurricane Bud—not Hurricane Betsy or Barbara. The naming of all tropical storms after women had been criticized by feminist groups.

JUNE 8. Naomi James of Britain sailed around the world alone in a record-breaking 272 days. During the voyage aboard her sloop, *Express Crusader,* James set another record: the longest nonstop sail by a woman. This was the 14,000-mile (22,530-kilometer) trip from South Africa to the Falkland Islands.

JUNE 9. The Mormon Church said that it would allow black men to become priests. The church had previously excluded black members from its priesthood. Priesthood is a major part of the Mormon religion. All males are expected to become priests at the age of 12.

JUNE 28. In what is known as the Bakke case, the U.S. Supreme Court ruled against rigid racial quotas in college admissions. But it also ruled that ''affirmative action'' programs are allowable. Such programs give certain advantages to black Americans and other groups that have been discriminated against in the past. The Supreme Court decision is considered the most important civil rights ruling since school segregation was outlawed in 1954.

JULY 7. The Solomon Islands became an independent nation. The Solomons are in the Pacific Ocean, east of Australia and New Guinea. They had been under British rule for 85 years. □ The U.S. Naval Observatory announced that astronomer James W. Christy had discovered a moon in orbit around the planet Pluto.

JULY 25. Medical history was made when a 31-year-old woman gave birth to the world's first "test-tube" baby. The baby, a girl named Louise, is the child of John and Lesley Brown of Britain. She was conceived in a laboratory, from an egg taken from Mrs. Brown's uterus. From then on, the pregnancy proceeded normally. The success of the procedure offers hope to many women who have problems conceiving children.

AUGUST 6. Pope Paul VI died of a heart attack at the age of 80. He had been the leader of the Roman Catholic Church since 1963. (On August 26, the church's Sacred College of Cardinals elected Albino Cardinal Luciani of Venice to be pope. Luciani took the name John Paul 1.)

SEPTEMBER 17. Middle East peace talks, which had begun September 6, ended successfully. The meeting was sponsored by U.S. President Jimmy Carter. Israel's Menahem Begin and Egypt's Anwar el-Sadat agreed to the framework for a peace treaty between the two countries.

SEPTEMBER 28. Pope John Paul 1 died of a heart attack at the age of 65. He had been pope only 33 days, the shortest reign of a pope in 373 years. (On October 16, Karol Cardinal Wojtyla of Cracow, Poland, was elected pope. He took the name John Paul II. It was the first time in 455 years that a non-Italian was chosen pope.)

OCTOBER 6. The U.S. Congress extended the time limit for ratification of the Equal Rights Amendment. The new deadline is June 30, 1982. By that date, 38 states must approve the proposed amendment to the Constitution. The purpose of the Equal Rights Amendment is to give women legal equality with men.

OCTOBER 15.   Irene Miller and Vera Komarkova of the United States became the first women ever to scale Annapurna. Annapurna is in the Himalayas and is the 10th highest mountain in the world.

OCTOBER 27.   President Anwar el-Sadat of Egypt and Prime Minister Menahem Begin of Israel were awarded the Nobel peace prize for their peacemaking efforts in the Middle East.

NOVEMBER 2.   The longest space flight ever ended as Soviet cosmonauts Vladimir Kovalenok and Alexander Ivanchenkov returned to Earth. They had spent 139 days, 14 hours, and 48 minutes aboard the Salyut 6 space station.

NOVEMBER 3.   Dominica, an island in the eastern Caribbean, became an independent republic, ending almost 200 years of rule by Britain.

DECEMBER 15.   The United States and the People's Republic of China announced that they would establish diplomatic relations on January 1, 1979. There have been two Chinese governments since 1949, when the Communists came to power and set up the People's Republic on the mainland. Their opponents, the Nationalists, set up a second government on the island of Taiwan. The United States supported the Nationalists. But, over the years, more and more nations recognized the Communists. U.S. relations with the Communists improved during the 1970's. By establishing diplomatic relations, the United States would recognize the Communist government as China's only legal government. And it would end diplomatic relations and a defense treaty with the Nationalists.

14

HAPPY BIRTHDAY, MICKEY MOUSE

He is known as Topolino in Italy, Mikke Mus in Norway, Mikki Hiiri in Finland, Miki in Turkey, Micky Maus in Germany, Raton Mickey throughout South America, Mouse Pigg in Sweden, and just plain Mickey Mouse almost everywhere else.

And in 1978, Mickey Mouse celebrated his 50th birthday!

The famous little guy with the big ears is more than just another cartoon character. He has become a unique part of our cultural heritage. For generations he has held a special place in the hearts of people everywhere—both young and old. His face is possibly more familiar to more people in more countries of the world than any other face.

But despite his long career and his great fame, Mickey Mouse is still a rather modest and unassuming character, trying to laugh at and cope with the world around him.

▶FIFTY YEARS AGO...

It all began with Walt Disney, who created his first original animated cartoons in 1920. Soon after, he perfected a new method for combining live action and animation. Then came Mickey, who was born in Disney's imagination in 1928 on a train ride from New York to Los Angeles.

Mickey's talents were first used in a silent cartoon entitled *Plane Crazy*. However, before the cartoon could be released, sound burst upon the motion picture screen. And so Mickey made his screen debut in *Steamboat Willie*, the world's first sound cartoon. It premiered at the Colony Theater in New York on November 18, 1928.

With the success of *Steamboat Willie*, Disney added sound to *Plane Crazy* and to another silent Mickey cartoon, *Gallopin' Gaucho*. (As with all of Mickey's pictures through World War II, Walt Disney himself supplied Mickey's voice. In 1946, when Disney became too busy to continue, Jim Macdonald, a sound and vocal effects man from the Disney studio, took over.)

Mickey's skyrocket to fame didn't take long. His cartoons became so popular that people would ask if a movie house was running a "Mickey" before they would buy a ticket. Soon, theaters were displaying posters that read "Mickey Mouse playing today!" Audiences would often sit through a feature twice to see Mickey again.

In 1929, Mickey's popularity led to the Mickey Mouse Club, which met every Saturday in local theaters for an afternoon of cartoons and games. The several million Mouse

On November 18, 1928, Mickey made his screen debut in *Steamboat Willie* — the world's first cartoon with sound.

Mickey Mouse ⋅:⋅ ⋅:⋅ **By Walt Disney**

Soon Mickey was appearing in comic strips, on toys and other merchandise, and on TV.

Clubbers had a secret handshake, a special member greeting, a code of behavior, and even a special club song—"Minnie's Yoo Hoo."

But Mickey's popularity wasn't confined to the silver screen. By 1930 his likeness was appearing on dozens of items, including wooden toys, drums, rubber balls, rattles, cups and plates, soap, candles, glass figurines, bookends, puppets, and clothing. The first Mickey Mouse comic strip appeared January 13, 1930. The strip is still published daily in hundreds of newspapers. And the famous Mickey Mouse wristwatch, first manufactured in 1933, is now a much valued collector's item. Today, more than a thousand companies produce Disney character merchandise worldwide—from T-shirts to toothbrushes, encyclopedias to earmuffs. These items feature not only Mickey, but Donald Duck, Goofy, Snow White, Peter Pan, Winnie the Pooh, and dozens of other Disney-designed personalities.

The peak of Mickey's golden decade oc-curred in 1940, with his starring role in the feature-length film *Fantasia*. A major artistic innovation, it interpreted music in colors, shapes, movement, and story. The animation techniques, which were years ahead of their time, have never been matched. *Fantasia* also introduced stereophonic sound to theaters, an element not used by other studios until more than 10 years later.

During World War II, the Disney Studio suspended nearly all commercial activity and concentrated on aiding the war effort with training films, goodwill tours, and the designing of posters and armed forces insignia. Mickey played his part by appearing on insignia and on posters that urged national security and the purchase of war bonds. And, incredibly, the password of the Allied forces on D-Day, June 6, 1944, was "Mickey Mouse."

Following the war, Mickey returned to making cartoons. In 1947 he appeared in his second feature, *Fun and Fancy Free*, in which he costarred with Goofy and Donald

Mickey had the starring role in *Fantasia* — which interpreted music in colors, shapes, and movement.

Duck in a new version of Jack and the Beanstalk.

Through the 1940's and 1950's, Mickey made fewer cartoons, giving ground to Donald, Goofy, and Pluto, who were more flexible as characters. Mickey's evolution into a Disney symbol made it increasingly difficult to create story situations for him. If he lost his temper or did anything sneaky, fans would write in insisting "Mickey just wouldn't do that."

In 1955, Disney agreed to create an afternoon television program. That was the start of "The Mickey Mouse Club," which became one of the most successful children's shows ever. In 1977, "The New Mickey Mouse Club," featuring twelve new Mouseketeers, made its debut on television.

▶A MOST SPECTACULAR BIRTHDAY

To help celebrate Mickey's 50th birthday, Walt Disney Productions produced a 90-minute TV special on November 19, 1978, called "Mickey's 50." The program was the biggest birthday celebration in Hollywood history, and it traced the creation and career of Mickey Mouse and included highlights from his many films.

Both Disneyland in California and Walt Disney World in Florida held parades down Main Street in Mickey's honor, featuring floats and more than 50 costumed characters. Articles on Mickey appeared in major newspapers and magazines. Dozens of schools, clubs, even whole communities had special activities to celebrate the event. And an Amtrak train, called The Mickey Mouse Special, traveled from coast to coast carrying Mickey on a whistle-stop tour.

Now that Mickey has reached middle-age, we can look back and understand why the Mickey of the 1930's was so popular. He was a little guy, born out of the Depression years, who satirized people's foibles and taught them to laugh. Most importantly, he was a character who dreamed dreams that were shared around the world.

WALT DISNEY PRODUCTIONS

ASTOUNDING CASTLES OF CLAY

Have you ever heard of termites building houses instead of eating them? Well, if you were to take a trip to the plains of eastern Africa, you would see giant mounds, or earthen "castles," that have been built by termites no bigger than ants. Some of the castles stand 20 to 30 feet (6 to 9 meters) tall, and weigh as much as two or three huge elephants. Each castle is the home of millions of termites.

Actually, the termites live in underground chambers and use the towering mound as a ventilation system, or air-conditioning unit.

The tiny African termites, most of them totally blind, construct their astounding air-conditioning systems because they are sensitive to extreme heat. By building high "chimneys" filled with holes, they can regulate the airflow and the temperature of their homes. Each giant mound consists of a maze of tunnels, walkways, and arches. Cool air circulates throughout this maze and is directed to the chambers below. If the air is very hot, worker termites dig for water and squirt it on the inner walls, thus cooling their home.

Most of the termites in a castle colony are worker termites. They are the ones that build the castles. Their saliva acts like cement when it is mixed with the soil. Inside their earthern dwelling, the workers raise fungus gardens to provide food for the entire colony. The fungus helps the termites to digest wood, the most popular termite dish. Workers feed the digested wood to soldier termites, which are not able to feed themselves. The workers also take care of their queen.

The gigantic queen is the most important termite in the colony because of her ability to lay eggs.

Permanently sealed deep inside the clay castle, the fertile king and egg-laying queen remain in a termite royal chamber. The king is bigger than his workers. But it is the queen that receives all the attention. Four inches (10 centimeters) long and as thick as a hot dog, the gigantic queen dwarfs all the other termites.

Why is the queen so important to the termite society? The reason is her egg-laying ability. A termite queen can lay up to 30,000 eggs a day. The eggs are then stored in special chambers, or nurseries, until they hatch. The queen lays eggs regularly to replace termites that have been destroyed by weather or by enemies.

Termites are constantly threatened by many different enemies. The aardvark, with its long sticky tongue, is able to scoop up thousands of termites in one mouthful. And ants, one of their most feared enemies, can burrow deep into the mound and kill even the king and queen.

Soldier termites protect the society. These soldiers are sterile females with very large heads and powerful jaws. When attacked by invading ants, the soldiers can block a tunnel and kill their enemies. Soldier termites rarely venture outside, where they would be unable to defend themselves or to protect their queen.

The castles of clay that dot the African countryside may look like ruins of a past civilization. But they are the homes of a fascinating society—a society of termites that builds houses instead of eating them.

HANGING HEARTS

Here is a mobile that will add a touch of color to your favorite room. Hang it anyplace where it will move freely. It also makes a nice present for Valentine's Day or Mother's Day:

What to Use:

red self-hardening clay
heart-shaped cookie cutter
rolling pin
transparent thread

small cardboard box
red felt
ribbon or heavy string
scissors, needle, tape, glue, waxed paper

What to Do:

1. Put the clay between two pieces of waxed paper and roll it flat, just as you would cookie dough.

2. Remove the top sheet of waxed paper. Use the cookie cutter to cut out hearts from the clay. Near the center top of each heart, punch a hole with a pencil. Let the hearts dry and harden. (It may take several days for the hearts to harden completely.)

3. Hang each heart from a double strand of thread.

4. Cut a piece of felt large enough to cover the box, and glue it to the bottom and around the sides.

5. Thread a needle with the line from one of the hearts. Run the needle through the red felt and the bottom of the box. The bottom of the box should be facing downward, toward the hearts, when you do this. Tape the thread to the inside of the box. Repeat with the remaining hearts, but hang the hearts at different lengths. If you need to adjust the height of some of the hearts, carefully remove the tape holding that heart's thread. Adjust and retape.

6. With the point of a scissors, poke a hole in two opposite sides of the box. Push the ribbon through the two holes and securely knot each end inside the box.

7. You can now hang your heart mobile from a hook in the ceiling.

Variations:

You can make many different mobiles in this manner. Use cookie cutters of different shapes. Use different colors of clay. Paint designs or glue colored glitter on the clay after it hardens. Make a circular shape instead of a square from which to hang the hearts.

THE RETURN OF THE WINDMILL

People are rediscovering the windmill. They are fixing up and using old windmills. They are building new ones that look very different from the older models. And in 1978, a small ranching town in northeastern New Mexico made the headlines because of its windmill. The town, Clayton, became the first community in the United States to have a windmill supply part of the public utility's electricity. (This is the electricity produced by a company, called a utility, for use by all the people in an area.)

Why this new interest in windmills? The answer is simple: the energy crisis. The world is running out of oil and coal, the fuels that now provide most of our energy. As supplies of oil and coal decrease, their costs go up . . . and up. There is another problem with oil and coal—pollution. Burning them pollutes the air. Getting them out of the ground may cause water pollution and, in the case of coal, may leave the earth badly scarred and unusable for many years to come.

In contrast, wind is free; it doesn't cost anything. We will never run out of it, though there are periods when the wind doesn't blow. And wind power doesn't cause pollution. Thus, the windmill, which has been used for hundreds of years to pump water and grind grains, is now being redesigned and tested as a device to produce electricity.

▶HOW WINDMILLS WORK

A windmill has several important parts, but the part that catches your eye is the sails. There are many different kinds of sails. Some look like wooden shutters. Others are made of cloth. Still others have many-bladed metal fans. The Clayton windmill has two very long blades that look like an airplane propeller.

It is important that the sails be at the correct angle to the wind. Otherwise they will

Some sails are made of cloth, as on this windmill in Greece.

not turn or they will turn too fast. The person in charge of the windmill does this by turning, or winding, the mill. Depending on how the sails are attached to the mill, either the top or the entire windmill is turned.

The operation of a windmill is simple. The wind turns the sails, which turn the axle, or wind-shaft. As the axle turns, any machinery attached to its bottom end also turns.

The machinery may be a millstone used to grind corn, wheat, cocoa, pepper, or other substances. It may be a pump, used to bring up underground water. It may be a turbine, used to produce electricity.

▶ WIND POWER

The wind has always interested people. The ancient Greeks believed there was a god who ruled the winds. They called him Aeolus. He kept the winds in a cave on an island. When he wanted to, he set them free to blow over the land. The rest of the time, he kept them locked up so they wouldn't cause storms or hurt people.

No one is certain who invented windmills, or even when they were invented. Many authorities believe they were invented in the Middle East. There is evidence that windmills existed in Persia (now Iran) in the 7th century. Genghis Khan, the 12th-century Mongol who conquered most of Asia, was responsible for introducing this kind of windmill to China.

The earliest evidence of windmills in Europe dates from the 12th century. These windmills were quite different from those in the Middle East. It is possible that the windmill was invented separately in these two areas of the world.

For almost 700 years, windmills were very common throughout Europe. A 1768 map of Liverpool, England, shows the locations of 27 mills. In Holland, some 9,000 windmills were operating at one time. The mills became a favorite subject of painters, including the Dutch artist Rembrandt.

The development of the steam engine in the 18th century resulted in a decline in the number of windmills. Windmills became less

Windmills were once very important in parts of the U.S. This one, with a metal-bladed sail, still exists in South Dakota.

profitable, especially when they couldn't grind flour finely enough to meet legal requirements. Today, working windmills can still be seen in many parts of Europe. But they are not as important as they once were.

The first windmills in North America were built by people who went there from Europe. The Dutch, for example, built many windmills in New Amsterdam, which is now New York City.

Eastern Long Island had many windmills. In the late 1880's, these attracted so many painters, with their easels and other materials, that some farmers complained that they could hardly get to their own barnyards. Some windmills on Long Island and in other parts of North America have now become tourist attractions.

Windmills were once very important in rural parts of the midwestern and western United States. In these places, there wasn't enough river water for people and animals. So windmills were built that pumped water from deep within the earth. More than 6,500,000 windmills were built in the United States between 1880 and 1930. They provided water for homes, farms, fire departments, and the locomotives of transcontinental trains. But these mills, even with modifications, could not produce very much electricity.

In the 1930's, the U.S. Government began building transmission lines to carry electricity to rural areas from power plants far away. This electricity was very cheap. It was used to run appliances in homes, to grind grain, and to pump water. As a result, most of the windmills fell into disrepair. That's just what had happened around Clayton, New Mexico. And as old timers watched the town's new windmill begin to turn, they told stories about the old mills and how they worked.

▶PROBLEMS TO BE SOLVED

Building a windmill that pumps water or grinds grain is not difficult. But building one that will change wind energy into electrical energy is still a challenge. Scientists and engineers are studying ways to solve the following problems:

A Steady Supply. The wind does not blow all the time. And it blows at different

Clayton, New Mexico, is the first U.S. community to have a "wind machine" supply part of its public utility's electricity.

speeds. If a building depended entirely on windmills for electricity, there would be times when the lights, television, freezer, and other electrical appliances wouldn't work.

At the present time, the best way to avoid this problem is to have both a windmill and a conventional generator. This is how the Clayton system works. Any electrical energy produced by the windmill goes into the utility's electric system. This automatically cuts down the amount of electricity produced by the system's oil-burning generator. When the wind doesn't blow, the oil-burning generator produces extra electricity so that the town's needs are met.

High Costs. Electricity produced from wind machines such as the one in Clayton now costs about three times as much as that generated from oil. The wind may be free, but the machinery needed to harness the wind is expensive.

Scientists expect the costs to come down as the size of the wind machines goes up. Other improvements in the machinery should also cut costs. In contrast, the cost of electricity from oil and coal is expected to continue to rise.

As Canadian Prime Minister Pierre Trudeau stated, "the era of cheap energy is behind us . . . . Conservation of energy must become a way of life—in our personal lives, and in commerce and industry. Our ingenuity must be invested in alternate energy sources and alternate technologies which are oil-conserving."

The wind can become an important alternate source of energy. Windmills will never be able to supply all our energy needs. But by using them to provide even 10 percent of our electricity, we would save billions of dollars now spent to buy oil from other countries. And windmills would help conserve the world's dwindling supply of oil.

JENNY TESAR
Sponsoring Editor, *Gateways to Science*

ON TOUR: THE ARTS OF CHINA

China is the world's most populated nation. Almost one out of every four people in the world lives there. In all, the People's Republic of China (the official name of the mainland country) has more than 850,000,000 citizens.

For many years, the Chinese isolated themselves from the rest of the world. As a result, we knew little about the people and their everyday lives. Nor did we know about their art—their painting, music, dance.

Now things have changed. China has opened its doors. Westerners (people of Europe and the Americas) are visiting the huge country, and the Chinese are visiting us. They are also showing us examples of their rich culture. Two recent tours have been especially popular with people in Europe and North America. One was an exhibit of Chinese peasant art. The other was a touring company of performing artists.

▶THE PAINTERS OF HU-HSIEN

In central China, there is a county named Hu-hsien (Hu County). It is a lovely rural area, consisting largely of farms, small villages, and many streams.

About 20 years ago, many of the people of Hu-hsien began painting in their spare time. They painted during lunch breaks. They painted at night, after working all day on the farms or in offices. And they developed a style of painting that is different from art styles found elsewhere.

Most of the Hu-hsien paintings are landscapes. They show the peasants in their natural surroundings, doing their everyday work. One shows people digging a well. Another shows the gathering of bamboo. A third shows fishermen pulling in a net filled with fish. A fourth shows people running machines in a factory.

The paintings are very colorful and are filled with details. On first view, they look decorative and much like folk art of the Americas. However, unlike Western art, almost every painting has an instructional or political message. In one painting, for example, a straw hat bears the words, "Serve the people." A drilling rig in another paint-

Many of the Hu-hsien paintings show the peasants at work. Children, too, have jobs to do.

Everyone in China works together, and you will often see women working side by side with men.

ing has words that say, "In agriculture learn from Tachai [a model farm community]."

The titles of the paintings also tend to be instructional or political. *Electricity Comes to a Mountain Village, Celebration of Water Conservation Project, Scientific Farming Gets Results, Grasp the Gun Firmly, We Love Chairman Hua,* and *Every Family has Money in the Bank* are some examples.

The paintings always show workers who are happy and healthy—not sad or starving. The workers are always smiling. They smile while dancing and while chopping wood. They smile while pulling heavy carts and while hoeing the ground.

The buildings and land shown in the paintings are always clean and well kept. The people are always cleanly dressed, even while digging a well or planting crops. The machines look new and run correctly. And the fruits and vegetables growing in the fields are huge.

Perhaps these paintings, which show a nearly perfect kind of life, are the result of something said by the late Chinese leader,

Mao Tse-tung, in 1942: "Life as reflected in works of literature and art can and ought to be on a higher plane . . . nearer the ideal, and therefore more universal than actual everyday life."

In 1976, the art of the peasant painters of Hu-hsien went on exhibit in Paris. Since then, similar paintings have been exhibited elsewhere in Europe and in North America. Westerners have learned a lot about rural life in China by studying the paintings. Most farm work there is still done by hand, using tools such as those used centuries ago. There are some trucks and tractors, but missing are the gigantic machines found on the large farms of Canada and the United States. Not missing are women: whether digging a well, pulling carts, or gathering crops, the work is shared between men and women. This sharing of work, known as collective labor, is universal in China. Everyone works together to do jobs that need doing. The paintings show people working together for the good of all—not working alone for self-reward.

▶PERFORMING ARTS COMPANY

Differences between life and thought in China and in the West can also be seen in the performing arts. Americans had a chance to enjoy some of China's best actors, singers, musicians, dancers, and acrobats when a group of them toured the United States in 1978.

Called the Performing Arts Company, the group presented selections from various Chinese art forms. The variety of numbers on the program gave Westerners a hint of the rich culture to be found in China. There were folk dances and ballet. There was music played on traditional Chinese instruments such as the bamboo flute, the erhu (a two-stringed violin), and the pipa (a lutelike instrument). There were selections from the famous Peking Opera.

Again, there were often instructional messages and patriotic themes. For example, one song includes these words: "When you

In *Red Silk Dance,* the dancers gracefully wave long ribbons of bright red silk.

drink tea from our Red base, you will never forget our revolutionary tradition."

One ballet tells of a peasant girl who is being whipped by a wicked landlord. She is found and rescued by members of the Red Army. In *Laundry Song,* Tibetan girls wash clothes for soldiers, while the soldiers fetch water for the girls. In *Militiawomen of the Grassland,* a group of booted women dance behind a red banner, waving swords and guns. Whereas in Western ballets the dancers' hands are usually delicately opened, here they are closed into fists. While in traditional Western ballets the women wear tutus, here they wear work clothes or military outfits. But not everything has a political message. In *Red Silk Dance,* twelve dancers move gracefully across the stage, waving long ribbons of bright red silk.

Perhaps the most popular number on the tour—and one of the most popular in China, too—was a selection from the Peking Opera called *Monkey Makes Havoc in Heaven.* It is a story about the Monkey King and the Jade Emperor of Heaven. The Emperor does not invite the Monkey King to the Celestial Peach Banquet. The Monkey King is very unhappy and decides to get even. He goes to the banquet anyway, eats everything in sight, tosses around peach pits and wine glasses—and makes a big mess!

The Celestial Army comes after the Monkey King, but they are clumsy and he is clever. The battle is a wonderful sight to watch. There are lots of acrobatics and exciting swordplay. Of course, the Monkey King, with some help from the other monkeys, wins. To celebrate the victory, there is baton twirling. There are only three batons but you think there are hundreds—the batons twirl so fast that all you see is a huge blur on the stage.

Monkey Makes Havoc in Heaven is a spectacular number. The actors wear gorgeous costumes of silk and other rich fabrics. Their makeup forms exotic designs of red, blue, black, and white. And there is a great deal of action, much of it funny. The audience doesn't get an inspiring political message. But it is entertained—and impressed by the great artistic talents of the Chinese people.

Monkey Makes Havoc in Heaven is a spectacular selection from the Peking Opera. It tells what the Monkey King (*right*) does when he attends the Celestial Peach Banquet (*below*).

THE RENAISSANCE PLEASURE FAIRE

Every summer, in an oak forest north of San Francisco, a 16th-century English village comes into being. There are half-timbered cottages and colorful stalls. Gracious noblemen and their ladies, dressed in rich velvets and laces, walk along the streets. There are minstrels and jesters, too, and tradespeople selling wonderful toys, food, and clothing.

Suddenly, there's a loud cry: "Make way! Make way! The Queen is coming!"

People move to the sides. Some cheer, others bow, as Queen Elizabeth I and her entourage pass by.

Moments later, the crowd's attention is focused on a fire-eater. Nearby, a young maid plays a sad ballad on her harp.

These are just a few of the many activities that are part of the Renaissance Pleasure Faire, a yearly event that gives 20th-century people a chance to take part in the life of 16th-century England. The fair is much like

ones that took place in rural England in the late 1500's. At the end of the summer, the farmers and other country people would take a break from the hard work that made up their everyday lives. They would gather at the fair to see friends and celebrate a good harvest.

The present-day fair is produced by the Living History Centre. In addition, the Centre holds free workshops during the year at which people of all ages can learn Elizabethan dancing, Elizabethan language, and how to make clothes like those worn in England during the latter half of the 16th century.

Several thousand people work on the Renaissance Pleasure Faire. Some of these people set up the village. They assemble the town, put up tents, and carry in some 6,000 bales of hay, which are used as seats at the fair's theaters and rest areas. Some of the workers are entertainers. Professional actors, musicians, singers, dancers, mimes, acrobats, fire-eaters, and jesters provide continuous entertainment in the theaters and on the village streets. All these people are dressed in 16th-century costumes. Many visitors to the fair also wear costumes. They come as merchants and milkmaids, lords and ladies, rich folk and common folk. Other visitors wear modern casual clothes. Look around and you may see a child in T-shirt and shorts chatting with a child wearing a full-sleeved linen shirt, knee breeches, and a velvet cloak. One will be speaking American slang, the other Elizabethan English. One child may be nibbling on a jester cookie—a chocolate chip cookie that is wider than a large dinner plate.

They may wander over to the games area. There they can watch the sword fighting and the archery. Perhaps they'll make some candles at the dipping wheel or join in a dance. There are so many things to do. For when you travel 400 years into the past, "All the Faire's a Stage, and all those who gather in festive Spirit are its Players."

Listen to a musician...

... and attend a play at the Renaissance Pleasure Faire.

31

YOUNG PHOTOGRAPHERS

Today's young photographers are learning early that photography is not just a hobby but a real art form. They know that their work can be as striking and as haunting as the greatest painting or the finest poem. So they work hard to produce remarkable photographs like the ones shown on these pages.

All these photographs were winners in the 1978 Scholastic/Kodak Photo Awards program. And the young photographers who took them gained as much satisfaction from producing excellent photographs as they did from winning awards.

Hang Glider, by Chris Lombardo, 17, Reseda, California

Man's Best Friend, by Bob Fries, 14, Bellevue, Washington

Fantasy Sunrise, by Scott Headley, 16, Rochester, New York

Scrooge's Secret of Success

Donald Duck tiptoed silently toward his desk. As he approached his Uncle Scrooge's private office, he noted with a sigh of relief that the office door was closed.

"If I can just get by that door without Uncle Scrooge seeing me . . ." Donald thought.

Suddenly, Scrooge's office door flew open. "Ah-hah!" Scrooge ah-hahed.

Donald froze in mid-tiptoe.

"Late again, eh, Nephew?"

Donald opened his mouth to offer an excuse and then shut it again. He couldn't think of a single excuse he hadn't used at least a dozen times before. The fact of the matter was that Donald had overslept again. And that wasn't much of an excuse for being two hours late to work for the third time that week.

"I believe you know the motto of this company, Nephew," said Uncle Scrooge, pointing to a fancy framed sign on the office wall, opposite Donald's desk. In bold letters, the sign read:

> EARLY TO WORK
>   AND LATE TO GO HOME
> MAKES A MAN RICH!
>   (SCROOGE McDUCK WROTE
>   THIS POEM.)

"That's how I became successful," Uncle Scrooge said proudly. "I get to work early and stay late!"

Donald had heard Uncle Scrooge's "Secret of Success" lecture a hundred times before. "I'll try to do better, Uncle," Donald answered meekly.

"I suggest you do more than try, Nephew. Because if you are late one more time, you're fired!"

That left Donald depressed for the rest of the day. He knew he was in big trouble. Some people

can't ride a bicycle. Others can't whistle. Still others can't swim. And still others can't get to work on time, no matter how hard they try. Donald was one of the last. He just couldn't wake up in the morning, even after the alarm had got him out of bed.

That evening, at home, Donald sat silently in his easy chair, looking very uneasy.

"What's wrong, Uncle Donald?" Huey finally asked.

"Yeah, Uncle Donald," Dewey added, "you don't look too well."

Donald sighed a big sigh. "Uncle Scrooge says he'll fire me if I'm late to work again."

"Uh-oh!" said Louie. All Donald's nephews knew how hard it was for Donald to get to work at all, much less on time.

The clock on the mantlepiece struck eight. "Well, I guess you kids should be in bed," sighed Donald.

Huey, Dewey, and Louie all groaned. Suddenly Huey had an idea. "Why don't you go to bed now, too, Uncle Donald?" he suggested. "Maybe if you get a good night's sleep, you'll be able to get up early enough tomorrow morning!"

"Not a bad idea," Donald agreed. And Donald and his nephews all went upstairs.

"Goodnight, Uncle Donald," the boys called as they disappeared into their bedroom.

"Goodnight," Donald answered, opening his own bedroom door.

Donald put on his polka dot pajamas, turned back the covers of his bed, and was about to jump in when he remembered he had forgotten to set his alarm.

He usually set the alarm for seven o'clock, but tonight he decided it would be a good idea to set it a couple of hours earlier. "That'll make me wake up and get to work in plenty of time," he thought to himself.

With his alarm now set for five o'clock, Donald climbed into bed. Soon he was sleeping like a baby.

Down the hall, Huey and Louie were sleeping, too. But Dewey was still awake. He was worried about Donald. He knew his uncle too well to really believe a good night's sleep would get him up on time.

Dewey climbed out of bed, careful not to wake up his brothers. He opened the bedroom door quietly and crept down the hall to Donald's room. He slowly opened his uncle's door and listened. The sound of Donald's snoring filled the room. Dewey went quickly to the alarm clock beside

Donald's bed. Without noticing in the darkened room that the alarm had already been set back two hours, Dewey set the alarm back an hour.

"Maybe if the alarm goes off an hour early, Uncle Donald can get to work on time," he thought, as he made his way back to his bed. In five minutes, Dewey was sleeping soundly.

A few minutes later, Louie woke up. He, too, was worried about Donald. He lay there, wondering what he could do to make sure Donald got up early enough to get to work on time. And then he had an idea. He got out of bed very quietly, opened the bedroom door, crept down the hall to his uncle's room, and set Donald's alarm clock back another hour. Then Louie went back to bed and was soon fast asleep.

But, of course, Dewey and Louie weren't the only nephews who were worried about their uncle's keeping his job. Pretty soon Huey woke up, and did just exactly as his brothers had done—except that he set Donald's alarm back two hours, just for good measure.

Donald's alarm clock was now set to go off at one o'clock in the morning.

And it did!

More asleep than awake, Donald heard the alarm, leaped out of bed, stumbled downstairs and out the front door. There was only one thought in his groggy brain: "Get to work on time!"

Meanwhile, down at Scrooge McDuck's Money Bin, a light still burned in the office of the company's president. As usual, Uncle Scrooge was working late.

He drew out his pocket watch and flipped open the lid. "One-thirty," he said to himself. "Time to go home." Uncle Scrooge tidied up his desk top, closed his briefcase, and snapped off his desk lamp. He was just about to open his private office door when he heard the outer door open and close.

"Now who can that be?" he grumbled, and reached for the doorknob to find out. Then "Wait," he thought to himself. "The cleaning crew has already been here, so it's not they . . . oh, no! Suppose it's a burglar!"

As much as he loved his money, old Scrooge knew he would be no match alone for a determined thief. So very quietly he bent down to look through the keyhole.

"Drat!" All he could see was a wastebasket.

The old keyhole trick wasn't going to work. "How can I see who's out there without his seeing me?" mused Scrooge to himself, and he frowned in concentration. "I have it!" And he nearly snapped his fingers, but then remembered he had to keep quiet.

"There's a window in that outer room, and there's a window here in my office, and there's a ledge that connects them," he planned to himself. "I'll just step out onto the ledge, sneak over to the other window, and I'll be able to see the culprit."

Now Scrooge was a duck who spent almost all of his time in the office working, and almost none of his time gazing out his office window, so it wasn't hard for him to forget that the window ledge he was planning to step out onto was twenty stories up in the air.

Carefully and silently, Scrooge lifted the window and stepped out onto the ledge.

Unfortunately, Scrooge, like the miser he is, had been penny-wise and pound-foolish when it came to building maintenance—in this case, when it came to fixing a simple window. As he began inching his way along to the other window, he heard an ominous thud. His office window had slammed tightly shut behind him.

Poor Scrooge! Here he was on a narrow ledge, shivering twenty stories above the street at one-

thirty in the morning. Well, he thought to himself, he might as well do what he'd set out to do—find out who was burgling his money bin.

Back pressed to the wall, Scrooge carefully sidled along to his target. A light was now shining out into the night from that outer-office window. "So! He wants to see what he's stealing, does he?" raged the elderly duck. "The very idea—wasting my electricity!"

Cautiously, Scrooge peered in the window. What did he see? His nephew Donald, of course, still clad in his pajamas, and sound asleep at his desk.

"That nephew of mine will be the ruin of me!" Scrooge fumed. "If he's going to put all those lights on, the least he can do is stay awake to work!" And he began pounding on the window.

Donald, who had a hard time waking up in the morning, had an even harder time waking up in the middle of the night. So it was a few minutes before he remembered where he was and could figure out what Scrooge's furious pounding could mean.

However, it finally became clear to him that the pounding meant his uncle was clinging to a ledge outside a twenty-story-high window. Donald lurched to his feet and stumbled over to let Scrooge back into his money bin.

Still not too wide awake, Donald looked dumbly at his uncle, who was still sputtering with rage. Then the hapless Donald flinched.

"You ninny!" roared Scrooge. "I thought you were a burglar! It's your fault I got stuck out there on that ledge." Then it dawned on him. "What are you doing here at this hour, anyway?"

"Why, Uncle Scrooge," stammered Donald. "I came to work early. I was just following your advice," he added, gesturing to Scrooge's "Secret of Success" sign on the wall.

That silenced Scrooge for a minute. Then he remembered how infuriated he'd been to see Donald snoozing away at his desk with all the lights burning.

"Well, Nephew," said Scrooge McDuck sourly, "I have some more advice for you!"

LITTLE BOY BLUE,
   DON'T COME HERE AT TWO
TO SLEEP WITH THE LIGHTS ON—
   OR, BLUE BOY, YOU'RE THROUGH!

WHO'S HIDING?

Can you find the hidden animals in the pictures on these pages? Why are they hard to see?

When animals blend into their surroundings, it is known as animal camouflage. Camouflage helps an animal protect itself from enemies. It also helps an animal catch prey—the camouflaged animal can sneak up before the prey realizes it is there.

Camouflage usually has to do with color. When the colors of an animal are nearly the same as the colors of its surroundings, the animal becomes difficult to see. Consider the polar bear. It spends much of its time on large pieces of floating ice. It tries to catch and kill seals for food. Because the polar bear is white and blends in with the ice, it can sneak up on the seals. Imagine how much harder if would be for the polar bear to catch seals if it were brown or green.

Animals that live in northern lands often have two coats. In summer, weasels, snow hares, and Arctic foxes have brown hair. As summer ends, they shed the brown hair and grow white coats.

Flounders and some other flatfish can change their appearance to blend with sand, mud, or pebbles. This is done by enlarging or shrinking color spots in the skin. On a pale, sandy ocean floor, the flounder will be pale. If it moves to a spotted, pebbled area, it too will become spotted. Squids, octopuses, and certain shrimps and frogs can also change color quickly.

Some animals practice a form of camouflage called mimicry. This means pretending they are something else. There is a mantis in Malaysia that looks like a pink and white orchid. Insects searching for nectar suddenly find themselves under attack. At the same time, birds and lizards that would like to eat the mantis don't see it. They only see an "orchid."

There are tree-dwelling geckos that look like bark, and chameleons that look like dried leaves. The viceroy butterfly fools its enemies by looking like a monarch butterfly. The monarch butterfly tastes awful, and animals that have eaten one or two avoid it—and anything that looks like it.

The young mule deer blends into the forest floor. If it senses danger, it will remain absolutely still so that its enemies won't see it.

38

The spotted scorpionfish is almost invisible in the coral reef where it lives. This fish is also protected by very sharp spines.

In winter, the ptarmigan is almost completely white and nearly disappears in the snow. In summer, this same ptarmigan has speckled brown feathers that help it blend with the rocks of the tundra.

The coyote's yellowish brown coat blends in with the grasses. Rabbits and mice won't see it slowly coming closer until it is too late to escape.

Weasels that live in Canada and the northern United States are pure white in winter. This helps them hide from animals that want to catch them.

This geometrid moth caterpillar hopes its enemies will think it is a twig. By staying very still and keeping its body at a certain angle, it looks like part of the tree. This kind of camouflage is called mimicry.

The varying hare, or snowshoe rabbit, is another animal that changes coats with the seasons. In summer, it disappears into the grasses. In winter, it is pure white except for the tips of its ears.

This cricket frog is nearly invisible in the stream. Its brownish coloring and warty skin make it look just like a bunch of pebbles in the water—until an unsuspecting insect wanders by.

GIRLS IN SPORTS

The pitch comes in. The batter swings. Crack! A sharp grounder spurts past the pitcher toward second base. The shortstop darts behind the bag, neatly gloves the ball, and in a smooth motion whips it to first base. Out!

"Nice play, fella!" someone calls to the shortstop from the stands.

"That's no 'fella' " someone else says quietly. "The shortstop is a girl."

If the shortstop's only problem is that she is sometimes mistaken for a boy, then perhaps she is lucky. Little by little, girls have begun to play on previously all-boy teams, and many of them have met with problems more serious than mistaken identity.

The main problem that girls have faced is nonacceptance by boys. "Girls aren't good enough to play on our teams," is what some boys say. The fact is, however, that as more girls get involved in sports, many of them become as good as, or even better than, a lot of boy athletes. But this leads to another problem: some boys are afraid of being outplayed and "shown up" by girls. So the problem of not being accepted by boys cuts two ways: to some boys, girl athletes are "not good enough"; to other boys, some girl athletes are "too good."

▶ **THE PHYSICAL QUESTION**

"Girls aren't as strong or as physically fit as boys" is another argument against coed competition. But, especially at the pre-teen level, this just isn't so. Until the age of 11 or 12, girls are, on the average, bigger and heavier than boys. And physical fitness doesn't depend on one's sex at all. If you have the proper exercise, you will be in good physical condition, whether you're female or male.

There is no question that as boys and girls get older, the boys will, on the average, get taller, stronger, and heavier. If some pre-teen and early teen girls play coed football, what will happen to them as they get older? Will they still be able to play well against stronger boy opponents? Perhaps not. So in contact sports such as football and hockey, coed teams may also be rare.

But in other sports, the physical differences between males and females do not always favor the males. Women and girls are more flexible than men and boys. That is, they are more loose-jointed. This would give females an edge in gymnastics, for example. And some scientists claim that girls and women are less likely to be injured than are boys and men. Because of the structure of a female's body, some of her vital organs are better protected than those of a man. Being less injury-prone is a definite "plus" in any sport.

Women may, on the average, even have more endurance than men. This is hard to prove, but the evidence suggests that it is so. There are women marathon swimmers, such as Diana Nyad, who are among the best long-distance swimmers in the world, male or female. And women running in races of 50 miles (80 kilometers) or more have often done better than men runners.

▶THE SUCCESSES

Even with all the problems, many girls have done well on previously all-boy teams. Consider Tammy Lee Mercer. She played tackle for the Amherst Regional High School football team in Massachusetts. Tammy Lee was an excellent football player and an exceptional athlete who kept herself in fine condition.

Anne Babson, of Ipswich, Massachusetts, was the only girl on her junior high's football team. Barbara Potter was the number one tennis player on her school's tennis team in Watertown, Connecticut.

In Houston, Texas, 18-year-old Linda Williams played right field for her high school baseball team. She was no superstar, but she played well, and had a lot of support from her male teammates. But Linda left the baseball team in order to concentrate on girls' basketball and volleyball.

As more and more girls play on what were once all-boy teams, the obvious question comes up: how far will it go?

▶ THE FUTURE

Some coaches are afraid that if the best girl athletes play on boys' teams, it will be difficult to develop strong girls' teams. Other coaches believe that the best girl athletes should play in the same leagues with the best boys. And the not-so-good athletes, male and female, should play in their own leagues. Talent, rather than sex, would determine who plays against whom.

Perhaps that is what the future holds for coed sports. For preteens and young teens, the number of coed sports teams will probably increase. As the athletes get older, though, the teams may become all one sex, especially in the rough contact sports.

But who knows? Girls and women have only begun to discover what their athletic abilities are. Female athletes have been improving greatly in all sports. In fact, they are improving at a much faster rate than male athletes. So it may only be a matter of time before that girl shortstop gliding smoothly across the infield becomes the first woman to break into a major league lineup.

ROBOTS: COMPUTERS IN FANCY PACKAGES

The kinds of things that people do can be put into three basic groups. First, we do things that we enjoy or that will make us better people—such as taking piano lessons, studying for tests, and playing baseball. Second, we do things that need to be done but don't really make us better—such as mowing the grass, washing dishes, and taking out the garbage. Third, we do things that are dangerous or very difficult—such as handling dangerous chemicals and moving heavy machinery.

People have spent a long time trying to find substitutes for human labor that could do the boring, dangerous, and hard things that need to be done. We now have these substitutes for people. We call them robots. And the modern robot is really a computer in a fancy package.

Many people think that robots are a recent invention. This is not true. Robots have been around for thousands of years. The first robots were actually automatons (aw-TOM-uh-tons). The ancient Egyptians were said to have built figures that could move their arms. Steam was used to make the arms move. In the 14th century the Arabs built an automaton that filled a wash basin with water and later emptied the dirty water when the user had finished washing. People continued to build automatons. And as they learned more about science—especially the science of mechanics—the machines became very sophisticated.

In 1774, Pierre Jacquet-Droz, a Swiss, built an automaton that was so amazing that people came from all over Europe to see it. It was called "The Young Writer," and it was the figure of a young boy sitting at a desk. He would pick up a pen, dip it into an inkwell, and write a message several lines long. People could not understand what was happening. They thought it was magic because they couldn't see the system of gears and pulleys that made the figure work. Jacquet-Droz was arrested and accused of being a sorcerer.

In 1817, the writer Mary Shelley came to Switzerland to see "The Young Writer." The automaton gave her an idea. In 1817 she wrote one of the most famous books ever written—*Frankenstein*. We all know the story of the mad scientist who built a man out of body parts. Dr. Frankenstein's monster was an artificial man. But Frankenstein's monster showed us what could happen when artifical life went wrong. This is the difference between a science fiction robot and a real robot. The real robot does only what it is made to do. It does not have a brain. It does not think.

Books and plays continued to be written about robots, but the word "robot" wasn't used until 1921. At that time a Czech playwright named Karel Capek wrote a play called *R.U.R.* In Capek's play, robots were mechanical men designed to take the place of real men working in factories. Men decided that the robots would work even better if they had emotions like real people—if they could love and hate and cry and hurt.

"The Young Writer," an amazing early automaton.

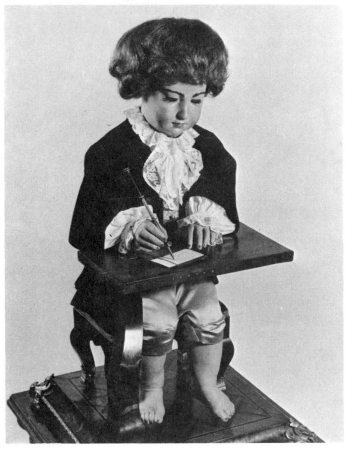

So these emotions were built into the robots. But, the plan backfired, and the robots took over. Their final act was to destroy all humans. The word "robot" comes from the Czech word *robota,* which means "work." Since 1921, "robot" has come to mean a machine that does the work of a person.

There have been many famous robots in the movies. Perhaps you know of the Tin Woodsman *(The Wizard of Oz),* Gort *(The Day the Earth Stood Still),* Artoo-Deetoo and See-Threepio *(Star Wars).*

Even though most of these robots are too fantastic to be real, there *are* real robots. And these robots can do wonderful things. In fact, Isaac Asimov, the famous scientist and science fiction writer, was so sure that robots would become a way of life that he developed the Three Laws of Robotics:

1. A robot must not injure a human being or through inaction allow a human being to come to harm.
2. A robot must obey the orders given it by human beings except where such orders would conflict with the First Law.
3. A robot must protect its own existence as long as such protection does not conflict with the First or Second Law.

▶MODERN ROBOTS HELP PEOPLE

Real-life robots do things that are helpful to people. Did you know that your family car may have been welded together by a robot? Have you ever made a phone call and gotten a recorded message? A telephone answering machine is a kind of robot.

Probably the most widely used robots in the world are the Unimates—industrial robots. A Unimate doesn't look like a TV robot. What you see is a large metal box that is about 5 feet (1.5 meters) square. This box contains the computer that controls the Unimate. A long, heavy "arm" with "fingers" at the end does the actual work.

Unimates are used in factories all over the world. They can put small pieces of metal together to make valves. They can move heavy machine parts from one place to another. They can pull hot metal out of furnaces. On an assembly line, a group of Unimates can weld the metal bodies of cars to the frames. A team of Unimates can make 450 welds in less than a minute. They

This robot can paint a ceiling, vacuum, answer the door, take telephone messages, and even "talk."

are all good welds, too. Some Unimates are still going strong after 65,000 hours of work. That's more than 30 years of man hours!

How would you like a job standing in the cold rain for eight hours, with cars and trucks zooming by? You probably wouldn't like it very much, but Silent Sam doesn't mind a bit. Silent Sam is another kind of robot that does useful work. He looks like a tall man. He wears work clothes and a hard hat, and he waves a red flag. But he isn't a man. If you get up really close you can see that Sam is made of plastic. Sam's job is traffic control. Operated by batteries, he can be placed right in the middle of a busy intersection or in the most dangerous spot on a construction site. He will direct the cars and trucks for 24 hours a day. His arms never get tired, and he doesn't get scared if a truck comes too close. Sam is popular with police departments, telephone crews, and highway construction companies.

Big Al is a brand-new robot, designed to guard banks. He is even taller than Silent Sam, weighs almost 700 pounds (318 kilograms), and is shaped like a cone! He doesn't wear a regular bank guard suit or carry a gun. But he is tough, and he is bulletproof. Here is how the people who build Big Al and his brothers describe how he works: "He has a humanlike voice. If you cross his path, he will demand identification. If you have the right ID, Al will let you past. If not, he calls "HALT." If you move more than 3 feet (90 centimeters), Al gives out a high-pitched scream that will make you think your head is going to ex-

plode. If you *still* don't stop, Al will grab you with his "hand" and hold you until the police arrive." By the way, his "hands" have a squeeze power of 1,000 pounds (453 kilograms). You can imagine that not too many bank robbers would want to take a chance if they knew that Big Al was around.

Unimate, Silent Sam, and Big Al are just a few of the robots designed to help make life easier for people. Have you read about any more? How about the Viking landers that searched for life on the planet Mars?

Would you like to build a robot? If you're handy, maybe you can. Jonathan Kaplan did it when he was only 11 years old. Now he's a teenager, and he's still building robots. His latest can do more than 200 tasks.

If you would like to try to build a robot, go to your local library or a computer store. They have books that will tell you how.

▶INSIDE A ROBOT

But before you start on your own robot, you must know what goes on inside those

Silent Sam is a robot that can direct traffic for 24 hours a day.

metal heads. A robot needs three basic parts. It needs mechanical devices to do the work. In simple robots these devices are usually gears and levers. More complicated robots have hydraulic systems. These are much like the devices that lift cars in garages. They operate by squeezing a fluid into a small space, creating a lot of force.

The second part that a robot needs is a sensor or a series of sensors. The sensors tell the robot what it is doing. Sensors may be as simple as "feelers" like those on an insect or as complicated as a TV camera.

Finally, the robot needs a "brain." Often the brain is a microcomputer. A human prepares a program that will tell the robot's mechanical devices what to do. The program is fed into the memory of the microcomputer. The microcomputer sends messages to the mechanical devices and thus makes the robot work. The sensors make sure that the robot is doing its job. They will inform the computer if anything goes wrong. If the robot is to do something different, a new program is written for the computer's memory.

So you can see that we really don't have to worry about robots taking over the world. They couldn't without the help of people.

JOHN VICTOR
President, Program Design, Inc.

Jonathan Kaplan builds robots. Would you like to?

THREE HOLY MEN

Saint Peter, the apostle of Christ, was the first pope. In the twenty centuries since Peter, 263 men have succeeded to his throne as leader of the Roman Catholic Church. In 1978 the world's 700,000,000 Catholics saw three men serve as *il papa* (Italian for "pope"): Paul VI, John Paul I, and John Paul II. Each of these three holy men, in his own way, well maintained the faith by which the Catholic Church has endured since the time of Saint Peter.

▶ PAUL VI

On August 6, 1978, the sad news was announced in Rome: *Il papa e morto*—"The pope is dead." Eighty-year-old Paul VI, who had been pope for 15 years, had died during the evening.

Born Giovanni Montini, Paul VI had been elected the 262nd pope in 1963, following the death of Pope John XXIII. He chose Paul as his papal name in honor of Christ's apostle Paul, who had carried the message of Christianity throughout the Mediterranean world. Like the apostle whose name he bore, Paul VI was a traveler—and he became known as the Pilgrim Pope. He was the first pope since 1809 to travel outside of Italy and he was also the first pope to board an airplane. He went to the Holy Land, to India, to New York City, to the Far East, to Africa, to South America. All his journeys were to promote world peace and understanding. During his reign, he made closer ties between the Roman Catholic Church and other Christian churches, such as the Anglican and the Eastern Orthodox. He also improved relationships between Catholicism and some major non-Christian religions: Judaism, Hinduism, Islam.

Paul VI led the Church during a time of great change. He presided over the Second Vatican Council, at which many aspects of worship were modernized. For example, Catholic masses are no longer conducted in

Paul VI: the Pilgrim Pope.

John Paul I: a short, popular reign.

Latin, but rather in the language of the congregation. Also, Catholics had for centuries abstained from eating meat on Fridays as an act of penance. But after the Second Vatican Council, "meatless Fridays" were no longer required of Catholics.

On most matters of Catholic doctrine, however, Paul VI insisted on retaining the original teachings of the Church. His 1968 message, "Of Human Life," reaffirmed the Church's position against birth control. Paul also maintained that only men may become Catholic priests, and he insisted on the tradition of priestly celibacy (the idea that the Catholic clergy may not marry).

Paul VI will be remembered as the man who stood before the United Nations General Assembly and said, "Never again war!" He will be remembered for his having wept when he saw the world's poor. And he will be remembered as a pope who held the Church together during a period of change.

▶THE WHITE SMOKE

When a pope dies, how is the new pope elected? The world's cardinals, the "princes" of the Church, gather at the Vatican, which is the residence of the pope and the center of the Roman Catholic religion. Hidden away from the outside world, they cast ballots until one cardinal receives at least a two-thirds majority. At times, the election process has gone on for weeks, months, or even years. But after the death of Paul VI, the cardinals chose quickly, electing Albino Cardinal Luciani on the first day of voting. The traditional signal, white smoke rising from a chimney on the Vatican roof, told the world that the Church once again had a leader.

▶JOHN PAUL I

It was a break in tradition. For the first time in history, a pope chose two names. He called himself John Paul I, naming himself after the two popes who had immediately preceded him. In choosing two names, he was telling the world that he would continue the work of those who had gone before him.

John Paul I was a modest man. Rather than a formal coronation as pope, he wanted a simple inaugural mass. Rather than be carried on a portable throne as other popes had been, John Paul I chose to walk. These, too, were significant breaks in tradition. John Paul I was showing that as pope he would live and act simply and remain close to his followers. He was thought of as a "pastoral pope," one who ministers directly to the needs of his "flock." And people loved him for it. Because of his joy and good humor, he was called the Smiling Pope.

John Paul II: the first non-Italian pope in more than 450 years.

Though in some ways untraditional, John Paul I was in other ways a conservative man. He insisted that Catholics maintain faith in the religious doctrines that had sustained the Church for centuries. He also believed that it was the duty of the Church to help the poor. But as a traditional churchman, he did not feel it was the duty of the Church to take part in political movements.

Sadly, the reign of John Paul I was very short. This man, who had touched so many with his smile and his simplicity, died only 33 days after his election, at the age of 65. For the second time in two months, the world's Catholics said good-bye to their pope. And once again, the cardinals came together to choose a successor.

The greatest break in tradition was yet to come.

▶JOHN PAUL II

When the white smoke rose above the Vatican on October 16, the news flashed around the world. For the first time in more than 450 years, the cardinals had elected a non-Italian pope. He was 58-year-old Karol Cardinal Wojtyla, from Poland.

Out of love for the two popes who had gone before him, he too chose the name John Paul.

The background of John Paul II may be very important in his reign as pope. Poland is a Communist country. Perhaps John Paul's election as pope is a sign that the Catholic Church will now seek better relations with the Communist world, even though as a cardinal, John Paul had criticized the Polish Communist government.

During World War II, the future pope worked against the Nazis in Poland. Since the war, he has had to live under Communist rule. He knows personally what it means to fight for human rights, and one of his first speeches as pope emphasized his concern for oppressed people.

John Paul II is athletic, intellectual, and good-humored. Like Paul VI and John Paul I, he is faithfully committed to the fundamental teachings of the Roman Catholic Church. He has lived with suffering, and many Catholics believe John Paul II will demonstrate the Christian ideal of the suffering servant of all humanity. The reign of the 264th pope has begun hopefully.

SUN DAY

May 3, 1978, was a day of celebration. In many countries around the world people gathered to honor one of our most important friends: the sun.

It was Sun Day. At the United Nations, people welcomed the rising sun with songs and dances. In Denmark, people toured houses heated by solar energy. In Japan, people learned how to build a device to collect the sun's energy.

And in the United States, President Jimmy Carter said he would increase the amount of money the U.S. Government spends on solar research. "The question is no longer whether solar energy works. We know it works," said Carter. In fact, he said he plans to install a solar hot water heating system in the White House.

The President also talked of the advantages of solar energy. Unlike oil and coal, the sun's energy is not controlled by a small group of countries or companies. It is available to people everywhere. And the sun's energy, as Carter pointed out, "will not run out. It will not pollute our air or poison our waters. It is free from stench and smog. The sun's power needs only to be collected, stored, and used."

Sun Day was organized by Denis Hayes, an environmentalist. In 1970, he had organized Earth Day, which focused on pollution. "Earth Day emphasized a problem," said Hayes. "Sun Day emphasizes a solution."

Sun Day had three purposes:

1. To increase people's interest in and understanding of solar energy.
2. To increase government support of solar energy research and development.
3. To decrease our dependence on nuclear energy and on fuels such as coal and oil.

There are many ways to use the sun's energy. At present, it is used primarily to heat water and to heat and cool homes Some 40,000 homes in the United States now have solar devices. By 1985 the number may reach 1,500,000.

Other buildings also use solar heating devices. A new fire station in Dallas, Texas, gets its heating, cooling, and hot-water needs supplied by 60 solar collectors on its roof. A public school swimming pool in San Antonio, Texas, is now heated by solar energy. And on Sun Day, the Anheuser-Busch brewing company introduced a solar device that heats the water used in making beer.

Robert Redford, the well-known actor, is an enthusiastic supporter of solar energy. Redford was one of the people who celebrated Sun Day at the United Nations. "The reason for Sun Day is to start making the solar dream a current reality," he told those who were gathered there. His dream is fast coming true, as more and more people are realizing that the sun is a very special friend.

The Iron Age volunteers built their community in England's countryside, far from civilization.

THE IRON AGE COMMUNITY

On March 31, 1978, a group of people in England "returned" to the 20th century. For one whole year, they had been living in the Iron Age of 2,200 years ago. They had lived without automobiles, pollution, frozen dinners, television, and almost everything else that commonly belongs to the modern world. They had gathered their own food, made their own clothes, and dwelt in a hut deep in the woods. Why? They were making an experiment in living the way the ancient Celts had lived, 200 years before the time of Christ.

The Celts (pronounced *selts* or *kelts*) were tribes that lived in western Europe beginning more than 3,000 years ago. They learned how to take iron from rocks and make it into weapons and tools. Therefore, the Celtic era is known as the Iron Age.

Many of today's Britons are descended from the Celts. That is why western England was a logical setting for the "Iron Age Experiment."

▶MADE FOR TV

The experiment was sponsored by the British Broadcasting Corporation (the BBC). In 1976, BBC television producer John Percival decided to make a series of TV films about how the Iron Age Celts had lived. He could have made films that showed only where the Celts had lived and what kinds of tools they had used. But Percival thought the films would be more interesting if they showed people who were actually living as the Celts had lived. He did not want actors pretending to be Celts. Instead, he wanted to film people who were living with all the problems, pleasures, and attitudes of the ancient Celts.

Percival put ads in British newspapers asking people to volunteer for the Iron Age Experiment. Over 1,000 people responded. From these volunteers, Percival chose six couples. One couple brought their three children. Among those chosen were students, teachers, a doctor, a nurse, and a builder.

52

To prepare themselves for the experiment, the volunteers first had to learn some Iron Age skills, such as weaving, blacksmithing, agriculture, livestock raising, carpentry, and pottery making. By April, 1977, the 15 volunteers were ready to go back in time 2,200 years. They settled together in Wiltshire, southwest of London. Far away from civilization, they lived in an Iron Age community.

Except for the TV camera team who came to film them every week, the volunteers were completely shut off from the outside world. Their exact location was kept a secret, to keep away curious 20th-century visitors.

▶THE CELTIC WAY

The volunteers worked hard at doing things the Celtic way. They used ancient tools to build the large hut that housed them all. The hut was made out of wattle (interwoven sticks and branches) and daub (a primitive plaster made of mud and animal hair), and had a cone-shaped roof. For clothing, they sewed animal hides and wove wool from their sheep. For food, they gathered wild roots and vegetables and grew their own peas, beans, and wheat. They made cheese out of goats' milk, and they raised hogs, cattle, and chickens for meat. They caught and ate squirrels, rabbits, and rats. They ground flour and baked bread.

Cooking had to be done over an open fire. It took a whole day to bake a loaf of bread.

Doing things the Celtic way wasn't easy. But the Iron Agers learned to adapt to their primitive way of life. Without soap, they washed themselves with clay. Without toothbrushes and toothpaste, they cleaned their teeth with twigs. Many British people are tea drinkers, and one woman especially missed her afternoon tea. So she learned to use substitute drinks made from dandelions or mint leaves. The doctor in the group learned to treat flu, headaches, and asthma with various roots, herbs, and barks. And he treated cuts and bruises with soothing honey from the group's beehives.

The volunteers weren't always sure they were doing things the way the ancient Celts had actually done them. They often talked and argued about what was "proper" for the Iron Age. When one man made a chair, he had to destroy it because Iron Age people almost certainly didn't have chairs. But just as real Iron Agers had done, they made their own dyes from barks and mosses. They entertained themselves by telling stories and by playing Celtic musical instruments such as the lyre (a stringed instrument), pipe, and drums.

The volunteers also tried to follow the religious beliefs and traditions of the ancient Celts. Instead of Christmas, they celebrated the Winter Solstice, which marks the first

day of winter. But they couldn't follow all the Celtic religious traditions exactly. For one thing, they didn't always know the correct Celtic prayers or chants. For another, the ancient Celts used to sacrifice one of their people as a way of asking the gods for a good harvest. None of the volunteers was ready to follow that particular tradition!

THE 20TH CENTURY—GONE BUT NOT FORGOTTEN

In spite of the volunteers' attempts to make everything authentic, the 20th century sometimes tried to poke its way into their lives. British building inspectors didn't approve of the hut as a living place, but they agreed to let it stand. British school authorities wanted the children to keep up with their lessons, so some 20th-century books and papers had to be allowed into the Iron Age. And animal protection societies insisted that the hogs could be killed only by "humane" 20th-century methods.

At times, the Iron Agers found that certain modern items were very necessary. The volunteers were allowed to use some 20th-century health devices, and an "outside" doctor came to the camp a few times during emergencies. Producer John Percival took the group for a short summer "vacation" at the seashore. While the vacation wasn't really necessary, it was probably a very welcome rest for the volunteers.

DID THE EXPERIMENT WORK?

How well did this group of modern people succeed as Iron Agers? Pretty well, it seems. They were able to provide all their own food and clothing.

Living together in a group had its problems, but the Iron Agers seemed to get along fairly well. Each couple had its own private area in the hut, but nearly everything was done in a group. You may wonder if any one person became the group leader. Apparently not. When the group was building the hut, the men gave directions and acted as leaders. But once the hut was built, day-to-day life centered around food preparation and household chores. Since the women were more experienced at these tasks, they acted more often as group leaders.

In time, the volunteers found that they were changing personally. They were walk-

Two volunteers prepare a meal over the fire, which was kept burning inside the large hut.

The group learned that working together requires co-operation and consideration of others.

ing and talking more slowly than they had in the 20th century. They learned that living in a group requires lots of self-control and consideration for others. And they also learned that Iron Age life was by no means easy. Most of each day was used for gathering and preparing food. Still, the volunteers had time to refine their skills in such Iron Age crafts as pottery making and weaving.

For the most part, the Iron Age volunteers enjoyed the experiment, but not always. In August, 1977, one of the men decided to hitchhike to a beach resort. Within two days, however, he changed his mind and returned.

In December the family of five left the community for good. One of the children was sick, and his parents insisted on taking him to a modern doctor. Five couples remained.

Some of the volunteers reported that arguments often arose within the group. One woman said that the arguments came up because without TV, books, and newspapers, the group had very little mental recreation. So they exercised their brains by arguing with each other.

▶RETURNING TO "NOW"

On March 31, 1978, the ten remaining volunteer Celts walked out of the Iron Age and returned to the 20th century. All were happy to come home. One of the women had especially missed her family and friends, chocolate, and her Bob Dylan records. One of the men had missed beer and cigars. The woman who had had to drink dandelion and mint tea could have her regular tea again. There were some 20th-century things that they hadn't missed at all—noise, pollution, and inflation. One of the women said that after a year in the woods, she didn't think she would ever want to live in a city again.

But for better or for worse, they were back. Producer John Percival had enough film for twelve TV shows for the BBC. And the volunteers had memories of a very unusual experience—plus $2,000 each, their "pay" for spending one year in an Iron Age community.

DANIEL J. DOMOFF
Consulting Editor
Educational Developmental Laboratories

CALCULATOR TALK

If you have a little pocket calculator, it can be more fun than you think. It will do much more than add 2 and 2. You can make your calculator talk to you! Well, almost. Would you like to get acquainted?

Multiply .3867 by 2. Do this by pressing down on the decimal point (.), then the digits **3, 8, 6,** and **7.** Press the multiply (×) button, then enter the number **2.** Press the equals (=) button. Now turn the calculator so that you are reading the answer upside down. See how friendly your calculator can be?

Here's some more calculator talk:

1. A person who is very messy is sometimes called a _ _ _ _. **(2 × 4000 + 75 =)**

2. If you want to see many different kinds of animals, go to the _ _ _ _. **(0.06 ÷ 3 =)**

3. A _ _ _ produces honey. **(151 × 2 + 36 =)**

4. When Santa Claus comes down the chimney, he says _ _ _ _ _ _. **(1.21212 ÷ 3 =)**

5. When it is raining and you have galoshes on, it is fun to _ _ _ _ _ around in puddles. **(50,000 − 4925 =)**

6. After a game of Monopoly in which he went bankrupt, Tom said "_ _ _ _ _." **(8775 × 4 − 29 =)**

7. A worm, a snake, and a fish are all _ _ _ _ _ _ _. **(5,000,000 + 500,000 + 37,000 + 937 =)**

8. Many people read the _ _ _ _ _ every day. **(113454 ÷ 3 =)**

9. If you scared a snake, it might rise up and _ _ _ _ at you. **(11 × 500 + 14 =)**

10. When you are making pancakes, the griddle will _ _ _ _ _ _ when it is ready. **(744430 ÷ 2 =)**

11. Children often get an upset stomach if they _ _ _ _ _ _ their food. **(47250 × 8 + 809 =)**

12. In school, the teacher tries to teach us to keep our handwriting very _ _ _ _ _ _ _. **(5 × 756200 + 937 =)**

13. You might very well still find an Eskimo that lives in an _ _ _ _ _. **(0.2373 ÷ 3 =)**

14. Before you can eat an _ _ _, you must break the _ _ _ _ _ _ _. **(1986 ÷ 2 =)(1546900 × 50 + 993 =)**

15. The girl was taking lessons to learn to play the _ _ _ _. **(4555 − 1475 =)**

16. When a person is sad, he or she might cry _ _ _ _ _ _ or just _ _ _. **(0.32064 ÷ 8 =)(900 − 95 =)**

17. The _ _ _ likes to _ _ _ _ in the _ _ _. ($226 \times 4 =$) ($18 \times 500 + 75 =$) ($1000 - 92 =$)

18. During a long rain, _ _ _ _ often turns into a lot of _ _ _ and _ _ _ _. ($5 \times 1421 =$) ($0.81 \div 9 =$) ($4821 - 1621 =$)

19. A _ _ _ _ _ is helpful to a student studying geography. ($9 \times 4231 =$)

20. The _ _ _ _ _ _ _ _ _ _ _ _ and _ _ _ _ _ the _ _ _ _ _ _ _ _ _ _. ($2754 \div 3 =$) ($4 \times 2002 =$) ($30449 + 1426 + 25832 =$) ($117048 - 63258 =$) ($14 \times 1589 + 12761 =$) ($17776 - 2666 + 19899 =$)

You may have figured out which numbers form which letters:

I	1
Z	2
E	3
H	4
S	5
L	7
B	8
G	9
O	0

Here are some more calculator words. Try to make your own sentence-puzzles with them. And make up some of your own words too. There are lots more!

be	38	hoe	304
beg	938	hole	3704
bell	7738	hose	3504
bless	55378	I	1
bliss	55178	ill	771
bobble	378808	leg	937
boil	7108	less	5537
boss	5508	lie	317
ego	0.93	log	907
else	3573	lose	3507
giggle	379919	obese	35380
glee	3379	oblige	391780
go	0.9	oil	710
goes	5309	sell	7735
gosh	4509	she	345
he	34	shell	77345
heel	7334	sigh	4915
hi	14	size	3215
high	4914	sleigh	491375
hill	7714	so	0.5
his	514	sole	3705
hobo	0.804	SOS	505

A Coat Tale

Pinocchio and his pal Jiminy Cricket hurried home from school. They were both looking forward to the warm fire that would be waiting for them at home, for it was late fall and already there was a hint of snow in the air.

Just as they reached Geppetto's shop, they met the kindly old woodcarver coming out of the door. "Go in quickly, Pinocchio," advised Geppetto. "Warm yourself by the fire. I must deliver this clock to Mrs. Benelli and then I'll be right back."

The little puppet watched his father hurry up the cobbled street. Geppetto was visibly shivering and hugging his arms close to his body. "I wonder why he didn't put on his coat," mused Pinocchio, closing the door.

"Don't you remember?" reminded Jiminy. "He sold it to buy your schoolbooks."

"Oh, dear," said Pinocchio. "Poor Father!" The little puppet began to pace in front of the hearth, a frown of concentration on his face. Then he smiled. "I know! I'll get him another coat!"

"What will you use to buy it?" asked Jiminy.

"I'll earn the money," replied Pinocchio with confidence.

The next few days the little puppet was often away from home. In the morning before school he swept floors for Mr. Gianni, the baker. After school he chopped wood for Mrs. Scalini and Mrs. Contini and old Mr. Tomaso. He delivered groceries for Mr. Montaro, the grocer, and he carried water from the well for Mrs. Navarro. Every time he watched Geppetto leave the warmth of his cozy shop on an errand, Pinocchio felt a glow of satisfaction. Soon his father would have a nice, warm coat.

After a week, Pinocchio took the money he had earned and went to the tailor. "Please, Mr. Agnelli, I would like to buy a warm coat for my father," he announced.

Mr. Agnelli looked at the small hoard of coins that the puppet put on his counter. "I am sorry, little Pinocchio," he said. "But what you have here will not buy a coat, even for one so small as yourself. You would need much more."

With a mumbled "thank-you," Pinocchio left the tailor's shop. As he crossed the square toward home, his steps were dragging.

"Cheer up, Pinoke," said Jiminy Cricket, trying to look on the bright side. "Just keep at it and you'll have enough for Geppetto's coat in no time."

As Pinocchio looked down at the coins—so few!—in the palm of his hand, and felt how cold the weather was already, he didn't notice that he was being closely observed by a certain J. Worthington Foulfellow.

"Ha-ha!" crowed the fox, with a sly grin. He poked his sidekick, Gideon. The cat was searching the pockets of his threadbare clothes for the price of a bowl of soup, and had found only holes in them.

"Aw, boss, I'm hungry," whined Gideon. "Why don't you think of a way we can cadge a meal?"

"That's what I'm doing, you fool," replied the fox. "Look—over there! It's that dumb puppet, and he's got a handful of money."

Gideon was skeptical. "He sure won't give it to *us*," he remarked. "He's probably still sore about that deal we made with Stromboli. Besides, his buggy friend is with him, and he's on to us for sure."

"Details," replied Foulfellow airily. "If we get rid of the beetle for a while, Pinocchio'll be putty in our hands. You just talk to him and keep his attention for a minute, and I'll take care of the cricket."

When Pinocchio saw the two con men ap-proaching him, he quickly stuck his hand in his pocket and tried to ignore them.

"Just a moment, my lad," called the fox. "We'd like a word with you."

Eying the pair distrustfully, Pinocchio backed away a few steps. "Now, now, kid," soothed Gideon. "Let's let bygones be bygones."

"Yes, dear lad," said Foulfellow, sweeping off his hat and dropping it neatly over Jiminy Cricket. "Of course the life of the theater isn't for an intelligent lad like yourself. You're meant for bigger things—like investing." The crafty fox held his hat in place over the unfortunate Jiminy with his toe.

Pinocchio looked at the fox. "What does investing mean?"

"I'm glad you asked that, son," replied Foulfellow, placing his hand on the puppet's shoulder. "Investing is making your money grow. Here, why don't we take a little stroll while I explain what it's all about."

"Hey, boss—your hat," reminded Gideon.

"Oh, that," said the fox. And he scooped his

hat up off the ground, Jiminy and all, and stuffed it on his head. The poor cricket tried to get Pinocchio's attention, but the puppet had forgotten all about him. Foulfellow and Gideon kept up a steady stream of loud conversation, drowning out Jiminy's muffled cries for help.

The two con men guided Pinocchio toward an empty field at the edge of town, all the time explaining how simple it was to "make your money grow." The puppet began to thoughtfully finger the coins in his pocket.

"So, you see, my boy," finished Foulfellow, holding his hat on firmly with one hand and gesturing expansively with the other, "investing is the career for you."

"I do have a little money," offered Pinocchio, pulling the coins from his pocket. "Tell me how I can make it grow."

J. Worthington Foulfellow glanced around carefully. There were too many people around to just take the money and run. Besides, he was opposed to exerting himself, so he improvised. "See this field?" he said. "Now, I wouldn't tell this to just anyone, but I like you." The fox leaned down. "This is a magic field," he confided. "If you plant those coins by the light of the full moon—which is tonight—they will grow into money trees by morning!"

Pinocchio was overjoyed. What a fine coat he could buy for Geppetto now—one with a fine, warm fur lining. "How can I thank you?" he cried.

"Don't worry about that," answered Foulfellow. "I can see you're happy and that's payment enough. We'll be going now," he added. "Good planting!" J. Worthington Foulfellow and Gideon the Cat went off to take a nap while they waited for Pinocchio to bury his money. They had every intention of returning to dig the money up later that night.

Jiminy had decided to lie low under the fox's hat and wait for his chance to escape. He felt it when Foulfellow lay down, and soon heard him begin to snore. Cautiously, the cricket lifted the edge of the hat. The coast was clear. So Jiminy hopped to the ground and hurried off to the "magic field."

Pinocchio, meanwhile, had finished burying his coins and gone home to pass a restless night waiting for his money to sprout. When Jiminy arrived at the field, the few little mounds where Pinocchio had planted his money were easily visible in the bright moonlight.

Jiminy quickly set to work to dig up his friend's

hard-earned money. He also thought he'd teach the fox and the cat a lesson.

Early the next morning, Foulfellow and Gideon, having napped rather longer than they'd intended, hurried to the "magic field." When they arrived, the stared in dismay. All over the field were hundreds of little mounds that looked exactly like hundreds of little places where one might have planted a coin.

"Curses!" cried the fox, thinking that he'd have to exert himself after all and dig up each mound just to find Pinocchio's few coins.

"Uh . . . boss—" warned Gideon, "here comes that puppet, and he's got the woodcarver with him."

"Curses!" repeated J. Worthington Foulfellow. "Time for us to disappear." And the two would-be con men snuck off into the still-dark village streets.

Pinocchio, of course, had told Geppetto of his grand scheme, and had brought him out to the

people have ordered for Christmas, I can easily afford a new coat. In fact, I ordered one just yesterday.''

"Oh," replied Pinocchio. And he was silent a few moments, still disappointed at the failure of his grand scheme. Then he heard Jiminy's small voice. "Cheer up, Pinoke. At least you didn't lose your money."

Suddenly the little puppet smiled. "Thanks to you, Jiminy," he said. "And I think I know just what to do with it."

Jiminy Cricket looked puzzled, but Pinocchio just laughed. "Come on, Jiminy," he said. "Let's go see Mr. Agnelli."

"The tailor?" the cricket asked. "But Geppetto already has a new coat."

"I know," said Pinocchio, "but I think I have just about enough money here to buy a cricket-size coat for the very best friend a fellow ever had."

"magic field" to see how his money had grown. The poor puppet's face fell when he saw the empty field.

Then a voice piped up from behind one of the mounds. "Well, Pinoke," said his Official Conscience, "I hope you've learned a lesson."

"Jiminy!" cried the puppet. "I'd forgotten all about you!"

"I know," replied the cricket dryly. "But I didn't forget about you." And Jiminy pointed to the small pile of coins at his side.

"Oh, Jiminy," cried Pinocchio. "My money!" Then he remembered. "But it didn't grow," he said sadly. "It's still as little as it was." The puppet turned to Geppetto. "I wanted to get you a new winter coat, Father," he explained, "to replace the one that you sold to buy me my schoolbooks."

"Why, you dear little woodenhead," said Geppetto tenderly. "What a nice thought. But you needn't have worried. With all the new clocks

THE HALL OF REPTILES AND AMPHIBIANS

Did you know that:

• People eat pythons more often than pythons eat people.

• Many lizards can shed their tails, probably to escape danger. The broken-off tail continues to snap and jump, diverting the enemy while the lizard runs away.

• In Colombia, Chocó Indians use substances from the skins of certain frogs to make poison for their blowgun darts.

These are some of the things you can learn in the new Hall of Reptiles and Amphibians, at the American Museum of Natural History in New York City. None of the animals are alive there. But they are nearly perfectly re-created. For example, there is a Burmese python made of plastic. A real Burmese python, which is a very rare snake, was drugged and covered with plaster for about twenty minutes. This was the first time that a plaster mold was made from a living snake. After the plaster was removed and the snake awoke, it was given to a nearby zoo. The plaster mold was then used to make a plastic model of the snake. The model was carefully painted, scale by scale.

The hall has many displays that show how reptiles and amphibians look, and live, in their natural habitats. Komodo dragons (the largest lizards in the world) are shown devouring a dead wild boar. A huge loggerhead turtle skeleton hangs from the ceiling of its exhibit case, as if swimming through the ocean. A female leatherback turtle is shown laying eggs in a nest on a Florida beach.

Within many of the displays, there are "mini-exhibits." These explain the biology of reptiles and amphibians. They show how the animals move, eat, reproduce, use en-

Eye to eye: A youngster looks at a cobra, one of the world's most poisonous snakes. Nearby, there is an exhibit that explains how to treat snake bites.

Lunch time: This exhibit (*above*) shows the natural habitat of Komodo dragons. These animals live in Indonesia where, as you can see, they may feed on wild boar.

ergy, and ward off enemies. There is a caiman (a relative of the alligator) eating a frog—and a frog eating an insect. There is a salamander with gills, a snake with legs, and a flying frog.

Other exhibits describe the role that reptiles and amphibians play in human lives. Did you know that European exploration of the Americas would not have been possible without the green turtle? This animal was killed to provide fresh meat for explorers, who otherwise would not have had enough food for the long voyage across the Atlantic.

Reptiles and amphibians are among the most colorful and varied animals in the world. Visit the new hall, and you will learn all about their world.

CATCH A FALLING STAR

Have you ever wanted to hold a star in your hand?

Some scientists are doing just that right now. They are probing deeply into the secrets of a piece of rock that fell to Earth from outer space. This space material is called the Allende meteorite. It is already famous as a storehouse of ancient data about how the sun and the planets were formed 4,500,000,000 (billion) years ago. Recently scientists have discovered that Allende contains something more: substances that came out of other stars before our solar system was even formed.

Until the early morning of February 9, 1969, Allende was a nameless piece of cosmic rock, one of billions that circle the sun like miniature planets. On that morning the rock plunged into our atmosphere. Had Allende been the size of a pea or a golf ball, it would have burned up completely, making a brief "shooting star" across the night sky. But Allende weighed tons. Its passage through the air produced a giant fireball that lit up the night sky over northern Mexico. It even shed light as far away as Texas and New Mexico in the United States. As the light died, there were thunderous explosions as the meteorite broke up in the air. Then came the pattering sound of thousands of meteorite fragments striking fields and deserts in northern Mexico.

Allende quickly became one of the most-studied meteorites in history. Nearly two tons of fragments were collected from a stretch of land along the River Allende, for which the meteorite was named. Because there was so much material, many scientists could study the meteorite at the same time. And they did—many of them in laboratories set up to study the moon rocks that were to be brought back by Apollo 11 only a few months later.

Right away the scientists discovered something new in Allende: They found large white fragments that were made up of unusual minerals. And some of the minerals had never been found in meteorites before. These minerals were rich in such chemical elements as calcium, aluminum, and titanium, and they had been formed at very high temperatures. Scientists think that these white fragments were the very first solid matter to appear when the solar system itself began to form from a huge whirling cloud of hot dust and gas.

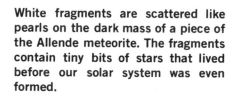

White fragments are scattered like pearls on the dark mass of a piece of the Allende meteorite. The fragments contain tiny bits of stars that lived before our solar system was even formed.

To have an actual record of the very beginning of the solar system was startling enough. But a few years later, scientists began to realize that those white fragments in Allende contained something even more exciting. Careful study showed that the oxygen in the fragments was slightly different from the oxygen found in other meteorites, moon rocks, and Earth materials. Allende contained too much of a kind of oxygen called oxygen-16.

Where had this extra oxygen-16 come from? Why hadn't it been mixed in with the normal oxygen that makes up other rocks and meteorites? Scientists began to believe that it must have come from some source outside the solar system. Perhaps the oxygen-16 had come from another star— possibly from a supernova that, in exploding, had sprayed its atoms into the dust cloud that was to become our own solar system. Trapped in the newly formed white fragments before it could be mixed or lost, some of this "extra" oxygen-16 was then caught up into the Allende meteorite and preserved for billions of years.

And there is an even more astonishing possibility. Maybe the exploding star ac-tually caused our solar system to form by sending shock waves through the original dust cloud, causing it to swirl and condense—and eventually producing the planets and the sun.

Now there is a frenzy of study as scientists try to see more clearly into this dim time before the solar system was formed. Within the last couple of years, high-powered electron microscopes have given a first look at what may be the interstellar particles themselves. Inside some of the minerals from the Allende meteorite are tiny bits of matter less than a thousandth of an inch in size. These are made up of even tinier grains of minerals formed at high temperatures and of alloys of platinum and other rare metals. This is a kind of mixture that has never before been seen in our own solar system.

What will we find as we probe more deeply into Allende and other meteorites? The work is just beginning. It will be a long time before we understand these tiny pieces of stars—stars that flared and died before the sun was born.

DR. BEVAN M. FRENCH
Author, *The Moon Book*

YOUNG ARTISTS

These lovely works of art are all from the Eighth International Children's Art Exhibition, which was seen around the world in 1978. Young people aged 5 to 15 from 65 countries sent in their artworks. A panel of Japanese art teachers chose which of the many entries would become part of the year-long exhibition.

The artworks that were selected were imaginative and unusual, rather than just skillfully drawn. They all show how young people from many nations see the world around them. If you look carefully at the pictures, you will see the differences—and similarities—in the ways people live.

To find out how to enter a future exhibition, write to:

International Children's Art Exhibition
2715 Columbia Street
Torrance, California 90503

Raking Autumn Leaves,
by Lisa Schimmens, 8, Canada

Untitled, by Lamio Fissal, 11, Qatar

Mr. Pot, by Albert Lake, Jr., 14, United States

Timbers, by Yoshie Hoyashi, 15, Japan

READY, SET—RUN!

You see them everywhere, it seems: on city streets, country roads, and suburban lanes; along the shoulders of asphalt highways and on narrow dirt paths in parks. Who are they? They're the runners and joggers—men and women, boys and girls, of all ages, sizes, and shapes. They run indoors, too. Take a look in any gymnasium, in any "Y." If you ask, "Where is everybody running to?" you've missed the point. Most runners and joggers only get back to where they started from. A much more important question than "where" is "why." Why is everybody running so much?

People have always felt the urge to run. It is a strong urge, probably dating back to the earliest humans, for whom running was a necessary technique of survival. But besides running to escape from enemies and wild animals, those early people probably also ran just for the joy of it. Your blood surges within you, your muscles stretch and strain, the wind hits your chest, and your lungs open to receive the air. Put simply, it feels good to exercise your body, and running is one of the best forms of exercise there is. But that is only part of the reason why so many people are running.

▶RUN FOR YOUR LIFE

Until about ten years ago, long-distance runners and joggers were not often seen in North America. Occasionally, you would see one or two loping through a park or along a roadway. People would hoot at them as they went by: "What are you, crazy?" or "Hey, Daddy Longlegs!" Almost all the runners were young men and boys, and most were members of school track teams. But there were also others, mostly older men.

They ran and jogged "to keep fit." They already understood what other people were just beginning to learn: the relationship between running, fitness, and health.

In the 1950's and 1960's, many Canadian and American doctors became concerned about the increase in heart disease. A well-known cardiologist (heart doctor), Dr. Paul Dudley White, began telling people that strenuous exercise was good for the heart. By "strenuous" exercise, Dr. White did not mean a Sunday afternoon game of softball or a round of golf. He meant exercise during which the heart beats fast for a long time, twenty minutes or more. The heart is a muscle, and to become strong a muscle needs strenuous exercise.

What sports offer strenuous exercise? The answer is, those sports that require constant motion and hard breathing. Basketball is good, as are handball, tennis, and soccer. But even better are cycling, swimming, cross-country skiing, and running. For cycling, though, you need a bicycle. For swimming, a pool. For cross-country skiing, snow and equipment. But for running, all you need is a very good pair of running shoes.

By the early 1970's, many people had become aware of the importance of strenuous exercise. They began to run. Some started with a mile (1.6 kilometers) a day but soon found that they could run even five miles (8 kilometers) daily. And the more they ran, the more certain things began to happen:

• They felt better, both healthier and happier. Running seemed to lift their spirits as well as make them stronger.

• Their hearts worked more efficiently. Their pulses, at rest, were slower and stronger. Those with high blood pressure often found that it dropped to healthier levels.

• They lost weight. Their bodies were trimmer. How fast they ran did not seem to matter. What mattered was that they ran, or jogged, regularly (at least three times a week) and that each run lasted for twenty minutes or more.

As time has passed, doctors have noticed a wonderful thing—heart disease seems to be decreasing in North America, especially among people who exercise regularly. Certainly, the decrease in heart disease is not

only due to running. But the general concern for physical fitness seems to have a lot to do with it. And so, just as the earliest humans ran for their lives in order to escape from enemies, many people today have begun to run for their lives—in order to escape, or at least lessen, the chance of heart disease.

Thousands of young people, from the earliest grades on up, have taken up jogging and running. But why should young people have to think about heart disease? It is because good health habits must start early. So, many schools in North America have started jogging programs in their gym classes. And the young people love it.

▶RUNNERS AND JOGGERS

What's the difference between running and jogging? Speed. But there is no clear line between the two. When most people first start, they just plod along as far as they can. After a few weeks, plodders become joggers. They go faster. They go farther. And then, at a certain point, some joggers become runners. But it is difficult to say just what that point is.

A good rule of thumb is this: while you're jogging, you can comfortably carry on a conversation. But if you have to gasp for air between words, then you're running.

The difference is not important. Both running and jogging are excellent ways to keep fit. A person who runs, though, may not only be keeping fit. He or she may be running in order to compete. The runner may want to race against other runners. Or the runner may wish to compete against herself or himself and try to beat her or his own best times over certain distances.

There are millions of joggers and runners in North America. Many have increased the distance they run to the point that they feel ready to take on the marathon—the most exciting long-distance race of all.

▶THE FINISH LINE

After the Battle of Marathon in 490 B.C., a young Greek soldier named Pheidippides ran a great distance to his city to tell of the victory. "Rejoice, we conquer," he gasped, and then he died. It is in his honor that the "marathon" race is named.

The marathon is 26 miles, 385 yards (42 kilometers, 352 meters) long. The course over which it is run may be hilly or flat, depending upon where the race is held. Actually the marathon is a "race" for only a very few of the competitors. Of the hundreds who may run in a marathon, only a few are actually good enough to win. For all the rest, merely finishing the marathon is considered a victory.

The best male marathoners in the world usually finish the race in about two hours, ten minutes. The best women marathoners, in about two hours, forty-five minutes. And for even the greatest runners, the marathon is grueling and painful. Even they cannot be sure they will complete the race until they have crossed the finish line.

People in their seventies have completed marathons, as have people under the age of ten. But in spite of how different they may seem to be, all marathoners have one thing in common: the desire to challenge their bodies to run despite the pain and to experience the joy of finishing.

▶PAIN AND JOY

Pain? Of course. Joy? Yes, joy too. To push your body to its limits—that creates pain. The joy comes from feeling your body get stronger and from going farther or faster than you have ever gone before. And sometimes there is a magic moment, when your breathing becomes easy, and when all pain disappears. You feel free. Your legs seem to move themselves, and easily and fluidly you glide on and on and on. At that moment, running is pure joy.

If you want to start running or jogging, follow these rules.

1. Get a medical examination first. Running is strenuous. Make sure you're in good health.
2. Get a good pair of running shoes. Running can be hard on the feet, legs, and back. Good shoes will provide cushioning and support.
3. Do warm-up exercises before each run.
4. Until you build up your endurance and strength, don't go too far or too fast.
5. Stick to it. Run at least three times a week.

A good running program is important in training for any sport. Running skills will improve your performance in sports like tennis, soccer, and basketball, and also in bowling and golf, where leg strength is the key to solid body support. A good running program develops upper body strength, too. Running and jogging help your lungs to process more oxygen, and your heart to pump more blood through your body. And there is another advantage to being in shape and feeling fit. When you wake up in the morning and feel in shape, and know that your training has paid off, you will look forward to competing—and to doing well.

Different sports, of course, require different types of running programs. A training program for basketball or tennis should be based on wind sprints, which cover shorter distances. Soccer or field hockey, on the other hand, require both wind sprints and longer, jogging-type distances.

Regardless of what type of running program you as an athlete decide on, you must go about it consistently. Sporadic training—where you run two or three times a week for a few weeks and then drop off to once a week and then go back to four times a week—just doesn't do the job. You must develop a program and then stick to it.

Personally, I like to run in the morning. I enjoy it the most then. Some people like to run after work or school because it helps them to get rid of the tension of the day. But it doesn't matter when you train, as long as you are consistent and diligent. After a while, you will find that you hate to give it up and, in fact, get more and more out of it. You will realize that you have put in a lot of work and feel very good for it. You won't want to see it all slide by.

I participated in track and field for twelve years before the 1976 Olympics. In 1970, I decided to concentrate solely on the decathlon. So for the six years from 1970 until Montreal, I worked every day of every month training for that event. For the last three years before the Olympics, I worked six to eight hours a day. I developed an athletic program that was strenuous without being boring.

I began each day at nine o'clock with twenty minutes of stretching. Then I ran for

an hour and followed that with light calisthenics. After lunch I did technique work for a few hours, some hard running, and finished up with weightlifting. I had to train that much if I wanted to win the decathlon. And in 1976 at the Olympic Stadium, all my work paid off. But, even if I hadn't won, it was all worth it. Because the Olympic experience was the high point of my life—and there could be no substitute for it.

BRUCE JENNER

TRAVELING TRUNKS

One morning, you arrive at school and see a large, old trunk in your social studies classroom. The trunk has a curved top and a big iron lock. You can tell that it has had hard use because it is scarred and worn. Would the trunk make you think of old letters? Of packing for camp? Or would you think of pirate treasure—of heaps of beautiful gold coins buried long ago? If you lifted the top of this special trunk you *would* find treasure. Not gold and silver, but the treasures of an American family. You would be looking into a West Virginia Heritage Trunk.

▶**A UNIQUE PROJECT**

The West Virginia Heritage Trunk project was designed to teach eighth-graders about their heritage, or their roots. The Children's Museum and Planetarium of Sunrise, Incorporated, developed the project for the West Virginia Department of Education. It helps students learn about life in West Virginia—as it was lived from 1863 to 1873.

Trunks filled with specially chosen items have been put together, and they travel from school to school throughout West Virginia. The traveling trunks are like traveling social studies textbooks. In each one, students find things that were used by the West Virginians of 100 years ago—things like clothes, toys, books, and family records. They are not the belongings of presidents, generals, or other famous people we usually read about in history books. They are the belongings of ordinary people.

This particular historic period was a special time because West Virginia had just become a state. It was also the time of the Civil War, when the country was divided and many people suffered great hardships. During this decade the war ended, and people worked hard to bring the states together again.

How would you go about learning how your family lived 100 years ago? Well, you could start with your parents. They will be too young to have been around, but they may remember stories that their grandparents told. If you are lucky enough to have grandparents or other elderly relatives, they will remember stories, too. You can also look through old photograph albums. Perhaps your family has other old records—birth certificates, diplomas, marriage licenses, letters, and death certificates. These, too, will help you learn about your family's heritage.

Talking and investigating is just what the Heritage Trunk people did. A team of interviewers traveled around West Virginia and talked with many older citizens. One woman, Fanny Cobb Carter, was interviewed just before her 100th birthday. Mrs. Carter had a very good memory. She even remembered Booker T. Washington, the famous black educator. He had visited her grandmother when Mrs. Carter was a little girl. Rebecca Morgan also shared stories told by her grandmother, a woman who managed the family farm and took care of her children while the Civil War raged around her. Her husband, an officer in the Confederate army, was killed in a duel.

When all the interviewing was finished, the team wrote the life stories, or biographies, of six families There were 36 people in these families. But the people never really existed. They were invented from all the information that the interviewers had gathered in their research. Their "lives" represent the lives of the ordinary people who lived more than 100 years ago.

▶WHAT WAS PUT INTO EACH TRUNK?

In addition to interviewing, some researchers looked for old trunks and for objects that could be put into the trunks. They searched through attics and basements and they shopped in secondhand stores. The trunks they picked had actually been used by early families as they moved from one place to another.

Here are some of the items that were selected to go into each trunk.

• A mountain dulcimer (DUL-suh-mer)—a musical instrument once common in West Virginia. A mountain dulcimer looks something like a violin without a neck. It is played by plucking and strumming the strings. Even today the strange sounds of the mountain dulcimer are heard as an accompaniment to blue grass and other folk music.

• A quilting kit. A quilt is a colorful blanket made from bits of fabric. Nineteenth-century women learned to make quilts when they were children. They used scraps left over from sewing projects and from worn out clothing. These people had very little money, so nothing was ever wasted. A quilt, in addition to being colorful, was thrifty. Students can actually make a quilt using the materials found in each trunk.

• Materials to make a sampler. A sampler is an embroidered picture. A hundred years ago, every young girl was taught needlework. A sampler was used to practice the various embroidery stitches. A traditional sampler began with a picture at the top. The picture was usually of the girl's home or her family. Below the picture was a verse, often taken from the Bible. The girl's name and the date were also worked into the sampler. First the picture and verse were drawn onto a piece of cloth. Then they were embroidered with colored threads. Some of the samplers were beautiful, with tiny, perfect stitches. Each trunk contains a printed sampler that can be stitched by the students.

• A mountain woman's wardrobe—two dresses (a simple calico for everyday wear and a silk dress with a lace collar that was worn on special occasions), a sunbonnet, a fan, and a pair of pantaloons. Women wore pantaloons under a dress to hide their legs from view. Nineteenth-century women were very modest, and it was not considered proper for legs or ankles to be seen. The clothes included in each trunk are for trying

A reproduction of an ivory fan.

A cornhusk doll.

A family of puppets.

on. But they are not authentic. They are reproductions. Girls and women from earlier times were much smaller than modern girls and women. Today's eighth-graders just wouldn't fit into the clothes that were worn 100 years ago.

• A working man's wardrobe—a pair of pants, a coonskin cap, and a wamus. A wamus is a fringed jacket made from the skin of an animal. If you compared the men's and the women's clothes, you would notice one thing for sure—women's fashions have changed a lot more than men's fashions. You would also notice that all the clothes were made from natural fibers like cotton and wool and silk. Our early relatives didn't have synthetic fabrics like nylon or Dacron. And the clothes weren't permanent press, either.

• Toys. The children of that period didn't have as much time to play as today's children do. They were expected to work—tending animals, gardening, cooking, and taking care of the younger children. Their toys were simple. Dolls were made from cloth and stuffed with rags. Corn husks, too, were used to make dolls. Each trunk contains a selection of toys, including a family of puppets.

• Documents. Every family had records that were kept at home. Often, statistics were entered in the family Bible—births, marriages, deaths. Each trunk includes copies of family documents, as well as of business records—a land grant, a doctor's leave of absence from a Civil War hospital, a shipping bill.

• A copy of the *McGuffey Reader* and a copy of *Noah Webster's Spelling Book*. These books were used 100 years ago to teach reading and spelling. You wouldn't find them much fun—there are few pictures and no color. School was serious business and, for most children, lasted only a few years.

▶HOW STUDENTS USE THE TRUNK

The trunk that arrives at a West Virginia school contains all the items just described. It also contains 36 cards. Each card describes a member of one of the six families. Look at the three sample cards on the following page.

74

These biography cards are used for role playing. In role playing, each student takes on the personality of another person. By "getting into someone's head" and by acting the way you think that person would act, you can learn a lot about that person. In this project each student becomes one of the 36 West Virginians and takes part in activities that these early settlers could have participated in. When you perform some of the jobs that the settlers needed to do just to survive, you will learn just how hard life was 100 years ago. When you attend some of their parties, you will realize that they also had fun.

Perhaps a student "family" might invite neighbors in for a spelling bee. The Webster's speller in the trunk could provide the words. There might be a simple prize for the winner. Not very exciting by modern standards, but it was probably a nice way for weary people to relax at the end of a hard day's work—during a time when there were no movies, no TV, and not even any electric lights.

All the families in a community might have a square dance. A hundred years ago, square dances were held in farmers' barns. The women wore their prettiest dresses. There was cider to drink and food prepared by the women. Nearly everyone attended, even small children. There was a fiddler to provide music and a caller to lead the dancing. Modern students might hold a similar square dance in their school gym.

Soapmaking is a long, hard job. It is dangerous, too. The soapmaker mixes melted fat and lye, a chemical that can burn the skin. The 19th-century family would save fat, perhaps for months. When enough fat had been collected, a day would be set aside for soapmaking. Enough soap to last the family for several months would be made at one time. A modern science class might try soapmaking.

It is possible to learn many things about the past by studying people's belongings and by role playing. This is just what the people who developed the West Virginia Heritage Trunk project thought. Thousands of West Virginia students think so, too. And maybe one day an antique traveling trunk will reach your school.

WHO ARE YOU?

You are **Carrie Brown** (September 10, 1862-1960)
You are the daughter of a slave now free and working in the household. You are being carefully brought up and taught by the women of the McNeill household. They teach you to read, teach you your catechism, see that you have proper clothing. You help with little chores such as dusting and sweeping. You are very much at ease in the household as a little girl, because the McNeills are interested in you. You are more fortunate than many other Negroes. You are to go to Storer College and become a teacher.*

* Parts of this fictitious profile are suggested by the life of Mrs. Fanny Cobb Carter as told in an interview.

WHO ARE YOU?

You are **Richard Abshire** (January 19, 1857-1939)
You are a farm boy who loves to know how things work. When your father got the beater, you were really excited. You are very interested in the water wheel at the grist mill. You made a water wheel in a smaller size. One of your jobs is to take the corn to the mill to be ground. Sometimes you take a little longer than necessary to do this so you can look around at the mill and at the blacksmith's shop too. The railroads are beginning to interest you.

There is no science taught in your one-room school, but your schoolmaster encourages you in learning how things work.

You love to eat—especially apple cobbler made from the apple trees on the farm. You live long enough to see great developments in machines and technology.

WHO ARE YOU?

You are **Rebecca Brown McNeill** (December 15, 1839-1905)
Your family came from England to the United States before the American Revolution. You are a determined woman capable of doing many things. While Dr. McNeill was away during the Civil War, you defended your house when a very much disliked southern general wanted to take it over. When you refused to turn it over to him and his troops, he said that he would return the next day and take it by force. He returned, but you stood firmly in the doorway with your children beside you. When the general gave the command to shoot at the house, his men refused to do so.* You also hid a slave in the corn stacked for harvest when the doctor felt he must sell her. When the steamboat arrived to take her, she was nowhere to be found.*

* These situations were suggested by the true stories told by Mrs. John Morgan about the life of her grandmother, Mrs. Littlepage.

NO MORE COWBOYS

Once upon a time, a cowboy was a cowboy and a stewardess was a stewardess. But now times have changed. Today a cowboy is a cowpuncher and a stewardess is a flight attendant.

Not too many years ago, people were expected to play certain roles in our society. Only men were thought to be able to herd cattle. Only young women were considered to be able to wait on airplane passengers. But today we accept everyone's right to choose whatever career she or he wants. Both women and men may become business executives or doctors or flight attendants or cowpunchers.

Some 20,000 different types of jobs currently exist. Until recently, the names of some of them implied that they were meant only for men or for women. The title alone may have discouraged a girl from becoming a repairman. And certainly a boy wouldn't want to be called a maid. But there are girls who want to have jobs where they repair clocks or telephones or cars. And there are boys who would like to work in and care for other people's homes.

To give everyone the same options in choosing a career, the titles of jobs such as repairman and maid—and cowboy and stewardess—have been changed. They have been changed to titles that do not stereotype the job.

Here is a career game for you to play. The numbered column (on the left) lists the old job titles. The lettered column (on the right) lists, in jumbled order, the new job titles. See if you can match each old job title with its new name.

Old Job Title
1. batboy
2. bellboy
3. brakeman
4. cameraman
5. cleaning woman
6. cowboy
7. deliveryman
8. doorman
9. draftsman
10. fireman
11. fisherman
12. flagman
13. housewife
14. maid
15. mailman
16. meterman
17. workman
18. repairman
19. sales girl
20. serviceman
21. stewardess
22. watchman
23. policeman

New Job Title
a. letter carrier
b. sales clerk
c. flight attendant
d. servant
e. cowpuncher
f. firefighter
g. drafter
h. bathandler
i. doorkeeper
j. cleaner
k. bellhop
l. braker
m. guard
n. flagger
o. camera operator
p. deliverer
q. police officer
r. servicer
s. homemaker
t. fisher
u. repairer
v. laborer
w. meter reader

ANSWERS: 1,h; 2,k; 3,l; 4,o; 5,j; 6,e; 7,p; 8,i; 9,g; 10,f; 11,t; 12,n; 13,s; 14,d; 15,a; 16,w; 17,v; 18,u; 19,b; 20,r; 21,c; 22,m; 23,q.

The new job titles you have just learned are hidden in this search-a-word puzzle. Try to find them. To find the names, read forward, backward, up, down, and diagonally. If you wish, cover the puzzle with a sheet of tracing paper. Then you can circle each title as you find it. One job title has been circled for you.

F	L	I	G	H	T	A	T	T	E	N	D	A	N	T
F	I	S	H	E	R	M	C	A	R	R	O	T	S	B
R	U	R	N	R	E	F	J	R	H	O	O	L	A	R
R	E	R	E	V	I	L	E	D	O	T	R	E	L	A
E	E	D	E	F	S	A	N	R	M	A	K	T	E	K
L	R	P	A	N	I	G	N	A	E	R	E	T	S	E
D	S	E	A	E	A	G	Y	U	M	E	E	E	C	R
N	E	E	H	I	R	E	H	G	A	P	P	R	L	R
A	R	A	R	C	R	R	L	T	K	O	E	C	E	E
H	V	I	E	V	N	E	E	C	E	A	R	A	R	T
T	I	D	C	E	A	U	R	T	R	R	N	R	K	F
A	C	Y	A	K	B	N	P	Z	E	E	B	R	N	A
B	E	L	L	H	O	P	T	W	S	M	K	I	Y	R
I	R	L	A	B	O	R	E	R	O	A	A	E	L	D
P	O	L	I	C	E	O	F	F	I	C	E	R	U	L

A Siamese Cat-Astrophe

Scamp was trotting round the corner of Jim Dear and Darling's house when his brother, Scooter, tore past him with a yelp and scurried into their doghouse. His sisters, Fluffy and Ruffy, were not far behind.

"What's got into you three?" called Scamp, poking his head into the doghouse.

"It's awful," wailed Fluffy, "just awful!"

"What's awful?" asked Scamp.

"Aunt Sarah's been here," moaned Scooter, "and she's left those troublemakers here for the weekend."

"Si and Am?" said Scamp. "Those cats?"

"Those cats," confirmed Scooter. "And I'm not leaving this doghouse until Aunt Sarah comes back to take them home."

"Me neither," chorused Fluffy and Ruffy.

"You mean that you three pups are afraid of two cats? What's so terrible about them?" Tramp's look-alike son laughed and bounded off toward the house.

Scamp peered in through the front porch screen and saw Jim Dear and Darling studying the two Siamese cats, who were prowling around the entry hall.

"I don't know if I like this business of taking care of these cats," said Jim Dear. "You remember what happened the last time they were here?"

"Looking after Aunt Sarah's cats is the least we can do for her," said Darling, "and you know how much they mean to her."

"Okay," said Jim, "but one swipe at the puppies and they go to a boarding kennel."

"I don't know what Scooter's so worried about," thought Scamp. "I'll see that those cats stay on their best behavior." Then a crafty smile lit his face. "I'll show them who's boss." He waited until Jim Dear and Darling had left the room, then nosed open the screen door and began racing in circles, barking.

The cats were unimpressed. Si gave a bored

ling were out, Si and Am slipped out an open window and appeared in the doorway of the doghouse.

"Look at precious puppies," said Si in a taunting voice.

Fluffy started to tremble. "Make them go away, Scamp," she pleaded.

"What's wrong, puppy? 'Fraid of we?" sneered Am. "You make good watchdog—if prowler very small."

"Leave us alone," growled Scamp.

"You brave in house where humans can protect—we see how brave you be out here," said Am, and he gave Scamp's nose a swat.

Scamp yelped in pain, then jumped at the cats. They were ready for him. They led him, snapping at their heels, up onto the front porch, through the small tear in the screen they'd enlarged by forcing their way. Once in the living room, Si and Am leaped up onto the back of the sofa, arched their backs and began to yowl.

When Jim Dear appeared in the doorway, Scamp was barking noisily at his tormentors, who were again doing their best to look scared.

"Scamp!" shouted Jim Dear. "What's got into you?" Then he saw the puppy-size hole in the front screen. With a disappointed sigh, he picked up the pup, marched to the doghouse, and tied Scamp up with a stout leash. "I hate to do this to you, fella," said Jim Dear, "but if you can't leave the cats alone, you'll just have to stay tied up until they've gone. It's only for a few days." He gave Scamp a consoling pat on the head, but it didn't make either of them feel any better.

Later that afternoon, Scamp saw the two cats peering out the window at him. They were wearing smug grins. "Mom was right," he thought glumly. "They're too clever and too mean for me."

And as if the cats' scorn weren't enough to bear, Scamp got a scolding from his mom and dad. It was a mild one, to be sure, but it stung, nevertheless.

The final blow to Scamp's self-esteem was being tied up while his brothers and sisters were free to play. As he longingly watched them disappear around the corner on their way to visit Uncle Trusty, Scamp spied the two cats strolling down the front walk. Si and Am glanced back at the leashed pup. "Shame, pup," called Si. "Not to chase defenseless cats." And they both snickered as they sauntered out the gate.

Scowling, Scamp watched the cats through the picket fence as they began to climb a tree. Then he saw something that made him smile. "The joke's

yawn, and Am a sly wink. Then the two cats gave two yowls and raced up the hat rack. When Jim Dear burst into the room, the cats did their best to look frightened. "This isn't going to work," said Jim Dear. "Those cats are going to a kennel."

"Now, Jim Dear," soothed Darling, picking up Scamp and setting him outside the door. "It's just for a few days. We'll just have to make sure the cats stay in and the puppies stay out."

"One last chance," sighed Jim Dear.

Scamp raced happily back to the doghouse to tell his story. He was nearing the end when a stern voice interrupted him. It was Lady. "Have you been near those cats? I don't want any of you to have anything to do with them. They're too clever and too mean."

"But, Mom," protested Scamp.

"No argument," Lady said firmly. "You can't get the better of them, so I advise you to stay out of their way."

Later that afternoon, while Jim Dear and Dar-

on them,'' he thought as he watched the dog-catcher get out of his van, carrying a cat-size net.

Scamp wondered if the dogcatcher had spotted the cats. "It would serve them right if they did get caught," he thought. "They probably don't know that dogcatchers pick up stray cats, too. And they are two very stray-looking cats."

The dog catcher quietly approached the cats with his net. Scamp wondered if he should warn them, but decided against it. Am had just begun to climb the tree and Si was about to follow, when, *WHACK!,* down came the net!

The dogcatcher pulled the angry, hissing cats away from the tree and held them securely in the net, a safe distance away from his body. "In you go," he said as he emptied the contents of the net into the back of his van. Then he drove off.

Dinner was late that night, since Jim Dear and Darling spent the better part of the evening searching for the missing cats.

"Poor Darling," sighed Lady. "She's so wor-ried about those cats. I feel sorry for her. I wonder what could have happened to them.''

Scamp looked up from his bowl. "I know," he said. Everyone stopped and stared at him.

"You didn't have anything to do with the cats' disappearance, did you?" asked Tramp.

"'Course not," answered Scamp. "I was tied up all day. But I did see the dogcatcher take them away.''

"Oh, the poor things," gasped Lady.

"Who cares?" said Scamp. "We don't like them anyway."

"Don't be so hasty," cautioned Tramp. "Jim Dear and Darling won't look for Si and Am in the pound. Without collars or licenses like you have, it's a one-way trip for those cats. I've been in the pound and I wouldn't wish that fate on anyone.''

Scamp's cocky mood faded. He felt even worse when Aunt Sarah came back for her cats and found them gone.

A sad procession left the house that Monday

afternoon—a sobbing Aunt Sarah carrying two empty traveling cases, followed by Darling, who kept dabbing at her eyes with a handkerchief.

"I should have warned Si and Am," thought Scamp. "I guess this is my fault."

The next morning, Scamp quietly slipped out the front gate. When he didn't come home for dinner, the household was in an uproar.

"I can't believe it," sobbed Darling. "First Aunt Sarah's cats and now Scamp."

"At least he has a collar and license," reminded Jim Dear. "We'll call the dogpound first thing in the morning."

It was a joyous moment for Jim Dear and Tramp the next day when the dogcatcher led a bedraggled Scamp down the pound corridor between the rows of cages and out into the waiting room. But instead of greeting his two rescuers with enthusiasm, the pup put his nose to the ground and ran back down the corridor, turning aside at the aisle marked "Felines."

"Scamp, come back here! What's got into you?" cried Jim as he chased after the pup. Scamp skidded to a halt in the middle of the aisle. As Jim Dear bent down to scoop him up, he glanced into a cage and stopped short. There, peering out from behind the bars, were two very frightened but familiar-looking Siamese cats.

"Why, it's Si and Am!" exclaimed Jim Dear.

A joyful reunion awaited Scamp when Jim Dear brought him back to the house. While Darling was calling Aunt Sarah to tell her the good news, Scamp's family plied him with questions. Tramp looked at his son with pride, for they all knew who was really responsible for rescuing Si and Am—even if Jim Dear and Darling would always think it was just luck.

"I guess it's too much to expect them to say thank you," said Scamp to his father, as they watched Aunt Sarah's tearful reunion with her cats.

"That's all right, son," replied Tramp, and he chuckled. "Think how much it must gall Si and Am to know they owe their freedom to a dog!"

SALTY PETS

"I bought some spotted sweetlips," said Barbara.

"My parents gave me a blackbar soldier," said Jimmy.

"I want a whitespotted puffer and a Moorish idol or two," said Kim.

It's hard to tell, but these children are talking about fish. They have a hobby that has suddenly become very popular. They have saltwater aquariums and are raising fish that are as colorful in appearance as they are in name.

Saltwater aquariums, as the name tells you, are ones that contain salt water, like that in oceans. Only ocean fish can live in these aquariums.

There are many different kinds of ocean fish. Some are very big. Others are tiny. Some swim in deep water, never coming near the shore. Others live among the coral reefs in shallow, tropical waters. Some are peaceful. Others often fight. Some are very choosy about food. Others can adapt to many different diets. Which are best for an aquarium?

Most people choose fish that live among the coral reefs. Coral reef fish are generally small, some only an inch (2.5 centimeters) or so in length. Most are less than a foot (30 centimeters) long.

Some of the coral reef fish are shades of gray, brown, or white. They quietly blend into their rock and sand surroundings. Others are the most colorful fish in the world.

Some fish are easier to raise in aquariums than others. Damselfish are recommended for beginning hobbyists. These are attractive fish and usually do not cost very much money. However, most damselfish have strong territorial instincts. That is, each one chooses an area and calls it home. It quickly attacks another member of its species that invades its "property." An exception is the damselfish known as sergeant major or prison fish. This yellow-and-black striped fish likes to move about in groups, or schools.

Most clownfish are also easy to raise. So are triggerfish, but they are fighters—one in a tank is enough!

If you would like to start a saltwater aquarium, talk to people who work in aquarium shops and pet stores. They will tell you how much it will cost to set up an aquarium and show you some of the fish you can raise. And they will explain how to keep the aquarium clean and the fish healthy.

Keeping a saltwater aquarium isn't as easy as keeping a freshwater one. But once you get the hang of it, you will receive a great deal of pleasure from the hobby. You will learn a lot about the lives and habits of saltwater fish. And you, too, will talk about sweetlips and Moorish idols.

Clownfish

Blackbar Soldierfish

Whitespotted Puffer

Masked Butterflyfish

CRAYON MAGIC

It's fun to learn about colors by using crayons. Each crayon will give you a different color, or you can experiment and make new colors, shades, and tints. By working with stencils and textured materials, you can achieve new and exciting effects. And you can draw on many surfaces—paper, fabric, sandpaper.

The tip of your crayon will make straight lines, curved lines, dots, dashes, and letters.

The end of your crayon will make perfect little circles, by pressing down and twisting.

Two crayons taped together will make straight parallel lines and curvy parallel lines.

Remove the paper from a crayon and use the side to make soft lines, as in the picture below.

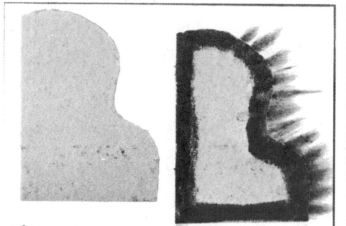

Cut out a shape from construction paper. Both the shape and the hole from which the shape was cut can be used as stencils. Crayon colors along the edges of a stencil can be "pulled out" with a pencil eraser (*above*). Stencils can be arranged under a piece of paper for a crayon rubbing (*right*). Stencil shapes can be repeated, overlapped, or used to create a whole design of many parts (*below*).

Apply a layer of black crayon over a design of many colors. Then, using the tip of a plastic spoon handle, scratch through the top layer of crayon to get interesting effects. You can scratch the design out in different directions (*above left*) or in one direction (*above right*).

You can place materials that have textured surfaces under a piece of thin drawing paper. Then carefully rub the side of a crayon over the paper. This textured print was achieved by using pieces of window screening, rubber mats, and rope.

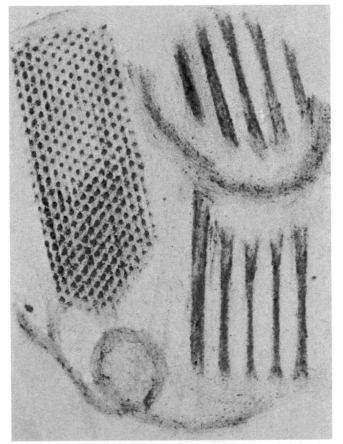

86

Try using your crayons directly on different surfaces. Textured papers, wood, fabric (*above*), and sandpaper (*below*) are some of the surfaces you can experiment with. Make big, bold pictures. Make small, detailed pictures.

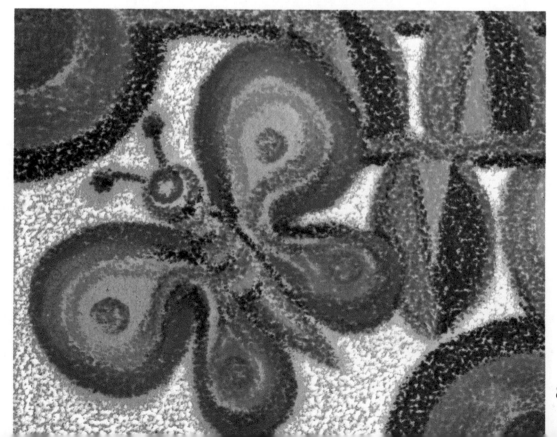

ENTRY TO THE TRAITORS GATE

THE TOWER OF LONDON

The Tower of London has been a fort, a palace, a prison. It once housed the Royal Observatory. For more than 500 years it was home to leopards, bears, and other animals of the Royal Menagerie. Today it is one of England's most important monuments and tourist attractions. People come from all over the world to see it and the treasures it contains. In 1978 the historic Tower celebrated its 900th anniversary.

Visiting the Tower of London is like walking through the history of England, for so many important events took place here. Perhaps best known is the story of two princes—Edward, Prince of Wales, and his brother, the Duke of York. The year was 1483. Edward was 12 years old; his brother was 9. Their father, the king, had died unexpectedly, and plans were being made for Edward's coronation as King Edward V. In the meantime the two boys were living in the Tower, under the protection of their uncle Richard. But Richard decided that he wanted to be king, and he arrested those

who opposed this move. The two young princes remained in the Tower after their uncle was crowned Richard III. Eventually the boys disappeared. To this day no one knows what happened to them, but many people think that they were murdered by their uncle. The Tower is no longer used as a prison. What is it like today? What treasures does it hold? Let's find out.

▶TURRETS, WALLS, AND MOATS

The Tower of London was begun nine centuries ago, in 1078, by William the Conqueror, who wanted to protect and control London. The first structure to be built was a stone tower, today known as the White Tower. It is the tallest building in the complex, with a basement, two floors, a gallery, and a turret at each of the four corners.

As the centuries passed, other rulers added to the fortress. A great stone wall with thirteen towers was built around the White Tower and its grounds. A moat was dug and filled with water. Later, another outer wall was built. The moat, now between the two walls, was filled in and a new moat was dug outside the fortress.

As you can imagine, the Tower became a well-protected place. Kings often lived there, especially during times of unrest. In fact, it was said that whoever held the Tower held the keys to the kingdom.

There were only two entrances to the Tower. One was from land, across a drawbridge. The other was from the Thames River. This was not an entrance that most people wanted to use. One guide at the Tower calls it "London's original one-way street." It was through here that prisoners entered the Tower—prisoners who often were on their way to the scaffold, where they were beheaded. (Beheading was a death reserved for royalty and the upper class. Poor people were hanged.) This entrance from the river is known as Traitors' Gate. Among the famous people who passed through the gate on the way to their deaths were Sir Thomas More and two wives of King Henry VIII: Queen Anne Boleyn and Queen Catherine Howard.

Above Traitors' Gate is a tower. Origi-nally it was called the Garden Tower, but now it is known as the Bloody Tower. This is where the young princes are thought to have been murdered. It is also where Sir Walter Raleigh lived during most of the twelve years that he was imprisoned in the Tower of London. Although a prisoner, Raleigh had a decent apartment and two servants to wait on him. He also had a little laboratory in a shed in the garden, where he did chemistry experiments. Raleigh's wife and son lived with him for a while, and he had frequent visitors, including Queen Anne and her son.

Raleigh had many chances to see the "beasts and birds" that were kept at the Tower. By the early 1800's—some 200 years after Raleigh's death—the menagerie had grown quite large. But in 1835 one of the lions bit a soldier. The Duke of Wellington, who was Constable of the Tower, ordered that all the animals be removed and sent to the new London Zoo.

▶THE CROWN JEWELS

The best-known treasures kept in the Tower today are the Crown Jewels. These

The most famous treasures kept in the Tower of London are the Crown Jewels.

Royal Sceptre, which contains a 530-carat diamond, the largest cut diamond in the world. There are the coronation rings, consisting of diamonds, rubies, and sapphires. There are gold and silver dishes used at the coronation banquet. And there are spectacular crowns, set with many beautiful jewels.

The Crown Jewels have been kept at the Tower since the 1300's. But they have not always been kept safely. Occasionally, a king would be in debt and would pawn some of the jewels. During the 1650's, England was ruled not by a king but by Oliver Cromwell. Cromwell sold or destroyed many of the Crown Jewels. Some of the jewels that survived were used in later crowns. The Imperial Crown of State, worn after the coronation and on other special occasions, contains some of these jewels. Altogether, this crown contains more than 3,000 jewels, mostly diamonds and pearls.

Another important crown is St. Edward's Crown, made for the coronation of Charles II in 1661. It is the heaviest crown in the collection, weighing nearly five pounds (2.5 kilograms). It has been used for every coronation since 1661. It is placed on the sovereign's head for only a short time, but it signifies that he or she is now ruler of England.

In 1671, Charles II was broke. He looked for ways to make some money. He decided to let "strangers" see the Crown Jewels. So you see, tourism is a very old business at the Tower of London.

▶THE ARMOR COLLECTION

Another tourist sight at the Tower that dates back hundreds of years is the royal collection of armor and weapons. Housed in the White Tower, the collection was begun by Henry VIII. Henry, it is said, had enough weapons at the Tower to equip 100,000 soldiers.

The exhibits show the changes that were made as years passed. There is body armor made of interlinking iron rings, which was worn in the early Middle Ages. It was gradually replaced by plate armor, which covered the body from head to toe—with matching armor for the warrior's horse! Weapons changed, too: clubs and crossbows eventually gave way to pistols and muskets.

are the jewels of the Crown—the person who is the sovereign, or king or queen, of Britain. Most of the jewels are connected with the coronation, the ceremony during which the prince or princess is made king or queen. They were last used in 1953 for the coronation of Queen Elizabeth II, Britain's current sovereign.

The Crown Jewels are very beautiful and extremely valuable. There are the Swords of Justice, which are carried in front of the sovereign during the coronation. There is the

The Ceremony of the Keys is enacted every night when the main gates of the Tower are locked.

▶TOURISTS AND RESIDENTS

Today, 3,000,000 tourists visit the Tower of London every year. Guiding them and safeguarding the Tower are the Yeoman Warders, more popularly known as the "Beefeaters." These men are members of the British Armed Forces and are easily recognized by their red and black uniforms.

At the end of each day the tourists leave and the gates are locked. This is done in a special Ceremony of the Keys. Carrying the keys and a lantern, a Yeoman Warder locks the outer gates. As he moves toward the center of the fortress, he passes the Bloody Tower. A guard challenges him:

"Halt! Who comes there?"
"The Keys."
"Whose keys?"
"Queen Elizabeth's Keys."
"Pass, Queen Elizabeth's Keys, all's well."

After being allowed to pass, the Yeoman Warder leaves the keys in the Governor's residence for the night.

The Yeoman Warders and their families live in the Tower of London. So do the Governor, the Curator of the Jewels, and others. Altogether, about 200 people call the Tower home. If they plan to visit other parts of London in the evening, they can return to the Tower after the gates are locked. But if they return after midnight, they have to know the secret password, which changes every day.

"It's very pleasant living here," the Chief Yeoman Warder told one visitor. "There're no peddlers or fear of theft. But it does get a bit noisy on days when we have 30,000 people coming through."

JENNY TESAR
Sponsoring Editor, *Gateways to Science*

91

ANDY GIBB: A SINGER IN HIS OWN RIGHT

Nearly everyone has heard of Robin, Maurice, and Barry Gibb. They're the famous Gibb brothers, better known to millions of popular music fans as the Bee Gees. But while the Bee Gees were busy climbing to the top of the music charts with the songs they wrote for the film *Saturday Night Fever,* another Gibb brother was making a name for himself. Andy Gibb, the youngest member of the Gibb family, moved from the shadow of his famous brothers to become a singer and songwriter in his own right.

Andy was just 20 years old when "I Just Want to Be Your Everything" became his first gold record. He followed that single with another hit, "Love Is Thicker Than Water."

His first album, *Flowing Rivers,* sold well over half a million copies. "Shadow Dancing," written by Andy and his brothers, became his third consecutive single and the title song of a best-selling album.

Andy Gibb grew up surrounded by music—and by his brothers' fame. He was born on March 5, 1958, in Manchester, England. His mother had been a singer, and his father was the drummer and leader of a big band. When Andy was six months old, his family moved to Australia, where his brothers started their music careers. Nine years later, the Gibbs returned to England. His first taste of fame came during this period—his brothers' popularity was so high that hundreds of Bee Gees fans gathered around the Gibb house every day.

But it was quite a while before the same kind of adulation was directed at Andy. He made his singing debut when the Gibbs moved to Ibiza, a small island off the coast of Spain. When he was 13, Andy was performing at local clubs on the island, receiving free cokes and food as his pay. And when Andy's family moved again (this time to the Isle of Man, an island off the coast of Britain in the Irish Sea), Andy formed a band that played regularly at local clubs.

Following the advice of his brothers, Andy returned to Australia to get his act together when he was 16 years old. He had planned to spend five years studying and perfecting his craft. But Andy's popularity with Australian audiences caught the attention of Robert Stigwood, the Bee Gees' manager. He invited Andy to the United States to make some demonstration tapes. And the rest is show business history.

Though greatly influenced by his brothers, Andy Gibb has a style that is definitely his own. "I like ballads," Andy has said, "but energetic as well as romantic, not dreary tearjerkers. They have to be up-tempo things, positive energy." He calls his own compositions "beagle"—a cross between the Bee Gees and the Eagles, another popular singing group. Whatever his music is called, Andy Gibb offers a positive note to the late 1970's music scene.

RIBBONS ROUND HER NECK

Ribbon jewelry is easy to make and fun to wear. It is also a perfect gift for birthdays and other special occasions.

Use your imagination to create unusual designs. Make a neckband to match a dress or to celebrate a holiday. Use nail polish or felt-tip pens to make a polka dot design. Use sequins to spell out "SUPERMOM" or a person's name. You'll quickly think of many other ideas.

What to Use:

Ribbon (velvet and grosgrain ribbons are especially nice)
Decorations (such as lace, rickrack, yarn, felt, pearls, and sequins)
Snaps (1 set for each neckband)
Scissors, thread, needle, chalk, glue

What to Do:

1. Cut the ribbon to the proper length. To do this, you must first use a tape measure to find the distance around the neck of the person who will wear the neckband. Then add about ½ inch (1.5 centimeters). For example, if the neck measurement is 13 inches (33 centimeters) make the neckband 13½ inches (34.5 centimeters) long.

2. Sew the snap onto the ribbon. This is used to close the neckband. The extra ½ inch (1.5 centimeters) of ribbon is for the snaps. Sew one part of the snap onto the end of the ribbon, on the *top* side of the ribbon. Sew the other part of the snap onto the other end, on the *underside* of the ribbon.

3. Decide what design you wish to make. If you want to use buttons, place them on the ribbon in different patterns. Keep rearranging them until you like the way they look. Then lift the buttons off the ribbon, one at a time, and use chalk to mark the position of each button. Put the buttons in a row on the table, in the order they will appear on the neckband.

4. Sew the decoration onto the ribbon. If you are using felt decoration, glue it onto the ribbon.

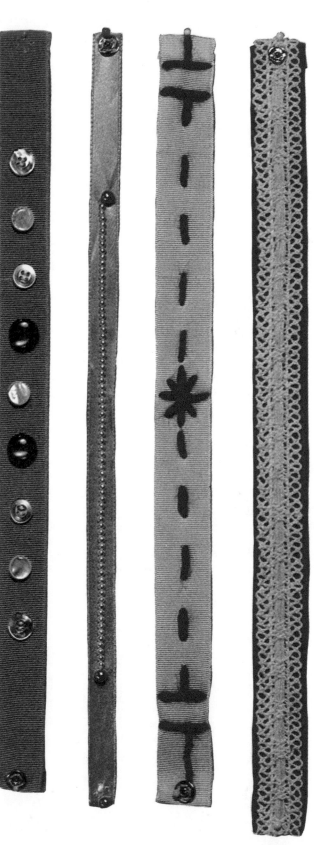

DON'T GLOP YOUR BELLYTIMBER!

Do the words in this title sound strange to you? You may not realize it, but you have probably been given just such a warning at the dinner table. The words mean "Don't gulp your food!"

The reason that "glop" and "bellytimber" are not familiar to you is because they are old English words that have become obsolete. Obsolete words are words that are no longer used. They are words that have died. At one time, "glop" and "bellytimber" were as common as our modern words "gulp" and "food." Now they are never used and cannot be found in current dictionaries.

How did these words die? Many words die when other words having the same meanings become more popular. And all of us contribute to the popularity of words by choosing some and rejecting others when we speak and write. "Glop" and "bellytimber" are only two of many words that were once alive but lost their popularity.

A word may also die if it describes a custom that has disappeared. For example, "flap-dragon" was a dangerous feat performed by medieval knights to impress their ladies. It meant drinking from a bowl filled with flaming brandy and bits of bread and raisins. When that custom died, so did the word "flap-dragon." When today's fads disappear, so will the words we use to describe them. In a few hundred years the words "skateboard," "yo-yo," and "bubble gum" may sound as strange as "flapdragon."

In 1978 we celebrated the 150th anniversary of the first American dictionary, *An American Dictionary of the English Language*. When Noah Webster (1758–1843) compiled this work in 1828, many words we use today—such as "radar," "motel," and "sweatshirt"—did not yet exist, and so they cannot be found in that dictionary. Similarly, many words that Webster included are no longer used today and, therefore, are not included in modern dictionaries. Because language changes rapidly, dictionaries are constantly being revised.

In the following story—"Who Stole Bartholomew-Pig?"—you will see obsolete and rare words used together with modern speech. All the strange words were once really alive and used in everyday conversations. "Bartholomew-pig" is one of those words that relate to a custom that became obsolete. From the 1100's through the 1850's, a fair was held in London on Saint Bartholomew's Day, August 24. There, a huge pig, called a bartholomew-pig, was roasted and shared among the townspeople.

After you have finished reading the story, try using a few of the obsolete words with friends or parents and see if they catch on. You'll be bringing an old word back to life again.

Noah Webster's dictionary of 1828 probably contained some of the words used in this story.

WHO STOLE BARTHOLOMEW-PIG?

The fair was at its height. Thrings of people strolled on the wong where younghedes announced games of skill and displayed eyebiting trantles for sale.

Roland Watson, the organizer of the fair, stepped out of the cosh he had set up as a temporary office to check on the fair. A multitude of sounds, smells, and sights made his ears, nose, and wink-a-peeps quop as he made his way through the mung. Cries of "Handmade muckenders and snotter-clouts!" and "Buy my ringos!" filled the air as Watson approached the main attraction—a platform that supported a huge bartholomew-pig roasting on a spit over a fire. Smiling confidently at the thought of sharing the pig with the townspeople at cockshut, as was the custom, Watson looked up at the platform and saw—nothing!

Where was bartholomew-pig?

Watson knew that Mr. Crawford had helped him set up the pig to roast earlier in the day. He tried to appear calm as he went over to a nearby booth to ask the younghede in charge if he knew what happened to the pig.

"Sorry, sir. I've been selling this lubber-wort so fast that I haven't had even a second to look up."

Then Watson questioned a vecke selling tuzzy-muzzies. "I wish that I could help you, sir, but I didn't even snawk it cooking. You see, I caught the gwenders a few days ago and my nose can't even tell the difference between these pissabeds and bunnikins I have right here."

"This calls for action," muttered Watson to himself. He rushed back to his cosh and summoned his afterlings.

"Now, don't make a whoopubb," he advised. "Something has happened to our bartholomew-pig. I don't know why some greedigut would steal it when there's plenty to share. But we've got to get it back by cockshut, as you know. So search every corner of this fair and go down to the brooling brook and even into the voil, if need be. Act quietly, don't get anyone alarmed by raising your stevens, and don't dringle. We'll all meet one hour from now at the platform. If you end up in a brangle, send an erendrake. We'll catch the breedbate who pulled this reak and give him a dose of his own slibber-sauce. Whisterpoops are too good for him!"

Roland Watson felt carked. He had one hour to search most of the fairgrounds on his own. "No time to indulge in mubble-fubbles," he said to himself. He walked over to the tent where pancarts announced the special events and called aside the flatchet-swallower. But he had no clues. Watson then questioned the animal trainer, whose blonke was drinking Adam's ale in the boose. But, again, no sign of bartholomew-pig. He talked to a bugle-bearded clown, a big man with fardry on his face who knew nothing but suggested that he wait and speak with two

crowds	
field/youths	
bewitching trinkets	
hut	
eyes/throb/crowd	
bibs/handkerchiefs	
candies	
animal to be eaten at the fair	
twilight	
snack food	
old woman/bouquets of flowers	
smell	
a cold and the chills	
dandelions	
spring flowers	
subordinates	
hubbub	
glutton	
babbling	
town	
voices/waste time	
state of confusion	
messenger/mischief maker/prank	
medicine/slaps on the ear	
anxious	
melancholy	
posters	
sword	
horse/water	
stall	
shaggy-haired/white makeup	

other clowns who were playfully yerding each other while the audience keaked and snirtled with delight. One clown with bright green painted murfles only shook his head when asked. The other clown, who was turngiddy from doing somersaults, only flerked his shoulders before running back into the ring.

> beating with a rod
> cackled/chortled
> freckles
> dizzy
> shrugged

Who stole bartholomew-pig?

Roland Watson had two more places to visit. The fairheaded bellibones at the farm-foods booth hadn't seen anyone sneak away in hudder-mudder with a cooked pig. They had enough to do just keeping the spiss crowd happy with nesh earthapples, homemade tipsycakes, and lulibubs. Watson's last stop was at the booth where poplollies were trying their skill at winning fartured dolls by chewing five dry crugs very fast and then whistling. Since most of them could barely wheeple, Watson found out no information from them.

> pretty
> girls
> secrecy
> dense/fresh cucumbers
> rum cakes/lollipops
> children (darlings)
> stuffed/crusts of bread
> a whistle with no sound coming out

"Barlafumble!" cried Watson as he walked toward the platform. The scrow was getting darker. A crowd had already gathered, getting ready for the bartholomew-pig feast. After Watson's afterlings reported no results from their efforts, Watson climbed atop the platform and announced, "My boonfellows, I have a merry-go-sorry tale to tell. Although this fair has been more iqueme than ever before, I am dretched to inform you that someone has stolen our bartholomew-pig. But don't be filled with ug. . . ."

> a cry meaning "I give up"
> sky
> good companions
> story both happy and sad
> pleasant/tormented
> fear

Just at that moment, a woman cried out from a distance, "Mr. Watson! We have the breedbate!"

Mrs. Crawford hurried to the platform. "I was watching the sunset through our eyethurl when I heard strange slurping noises just a wurp away. I ran over to the ha-ha nearby and saw a large dog glopping huge pieces of the bartholomew-pig. My husband arrived soon after and told me what had happened. He was the one, you know, who had prepared the bartholomew-pig on the pudding-prick. The pig was roasting nicely when my husband noticed it was about to fall off. So he carefully eased the pig off the skewer. As he rested it on the platform, a dog jumped up and tore the pig apart. But, no need to quetch. There will still be enough bellytimber for all! When I realized that we couldn't eat the pig, I yarkened a lot of food from our farm as quick as a thrip. My husband is coming toward us now with all of it on a wagon."

> window
> stone's throw/ditch
> greedily swallowing
> skewer
> moan
> food
> prepared
> snap of the fingers

"Mrs. Crawford! You are as precious to us as a bulse!" exclaimed Roland Watson, giving her a lip-clap. "This has been quite a darg for all of us. I am glad we have no magsmen among us. We are a voil of straight-fingered citizens! But a dog is a dog and we can't speak for it. If it wants to dig its flesh-spades into a roasted pig, we can't prevent it. But what we can do is cheer for the Crawfords who fellowfelt and helped us all!"

> purse of diamonds
> kiss
> day's work/swindlers
> thoroughly honest
> claws
> sympathized

SUSAN KELZ SPERLING
Author, *Poplollies and Bellibones: A Celebration of Lost Words*

A MUSEUM JUST FOR YOU

Use a windmill to pump water. Play "Chopsticks" on a calliophone. Run a steam engine and mill some grain. Examine a flintlock gun and an insect collection. Relax and listen to folktales.

At the Brooklyn Children's Museum, there are dozens of things to do and see. The museum, in New York City, opened in 1899. It is the oldest children's museum in the world. A few years ago, it moved into a new home that is mostly underground. And it has been designed just for you!

Visitors enter the museum through an antique kiosk that once marked the entrance to a New York City subway station. Then they walk down a ramp, into a long corrugated tunnel. This is the People Tube. In the tube and in nearby open areas are all sorts of displays and equipment. Visitors are encouraged to use machines, play instruments, climb inside a giant diamond, and look through microscopes. You will have many exciting, fun-filled hours at the Brooklyn Children's Museum.

This aerial bridge leads to the roof of the museum, where there is a Sky Theater.

You can operate this steam engine. By attaching various tools to the engine's drive shaft, you can make it do different kinds of work.

This insect collection is just one of the many fascinating exhibits found at the museum.

Children examine a collection of bones. In the background is a model of a diamond crystal — 8,000,000,000 (billion) times larger than the real thing.

The museum holds many workshops. Here, children are designing their own masks after having studied carved wooden masks that come from western Africa.

A stream of water runs through the neon-lit People Tube. You can operate pumps, valves, and other equipment, thereby raising or lowering water levels — or even stopping the flow of water completely.

These children are playing a drum from Ghana. The museum also has a Japanese zither, a Nigerian flute, and a New Guinea drum that is shaped like a crocodile.

MARCONI'S WIRELESS RADIO

On a brisk winter day in 1903, on a hilltop in southwest England, the Italian inventor Guglielmo Marconi and several assistants huddled around a wireless radio receiver. They were listening to the dots and dashes of a Morse code message being beamed to them from a transmitter on Cape Cod in Massachusetts—2,000 miles (3,200 kilometers) across the Atlantic Ocean.

The message on that historic day—January 19—was from U.S. President Theodore Roosevelt. It was part of an exchange of greetings between the American president and Britain's King Edward VII. And it was the first two-way transatlantic communication using wireless telegraph (or radio).

That scientific triumph is still honored today. The work of Marconi, who is often called "the father of the wireless," set the stage for the radio and television of today.

In January, 1978, the 75th anniversary of Marconi's feat was commemorated with a re-enactment of the event—on that same hilltop at Poldhu, England. On hand were Marconi's widow and one of his daughters. There were also groups of schoolchildren to share in the excitement, which included a wireless greeting sent from President Jimmy Carter of the United States. And there were other messages, in many languages, from all over the world.

It was back in 1894 that Guglielmo Marconi, then a young man of 20, first became interested in the idea of using electromagnetic waves for communication. At that time, the telegraph was the only way to send messages long distances. But the telegraph required wires on land and an enormous number of underwater cables at sea.

How marvelous it would be, Marconi thought, if all those cables could be replaced by a wireless telegraph. It would be especially helpful to ships at sea trying to communicate with one another or with land stations. So he left his native Italy and went to England, where there was more shipping activity. In 1901, Marconi accomplished what many thought was impossible. He sent the first transatlantic wireless signal from his station in England to a receiving station in Newfoundland, Canada.

Some people had argued that it couldn't be done. They believed that radio waves could only move in a straight line. But Marconi proved that radio waves could bend to follow the curve of the earth's surface. That discovery led to the development of radio and television.

Marconi received many honors, including the Nobel prize in physics in 1909. When he died in 1937, he had earned a reputation as one of the world's great scientific pioneers.

TAPETIME

Here's a quick and easy way to recycle glass bottles and tin cans. In just an hour you can make an attractive vase, candle holder, candy dish, or pencil holder. All you need is a clean can or bottle, a roll of masking tape, a pair of scissors, and some shoe polish wax.

Start by cutting small pieces of masking tape. You can cut the tape straight across. But for variety, you might make rounded edges. This will give a scalloped look to the finished product. Or, for zigzag edges, cut the tape with pinking shears.

Then put the pieces on the container, overlapping each piece, in an attractive design. Press each piece firmly to the glass— you don't want any loose edges. Make a clean edge around the container's opening. If you are covering a glass bottle, be sure to cover the bottom.

When you finish covering the container, apply a coat of shoe polish wax to the tape. Let stand for a few minutes, then rub with a clean cloth until the polish is shiny. Repeat this process several times. When there are four or five coats of shoe polish on the tape, you will have a rich, shiny surface—and a very pretty container.

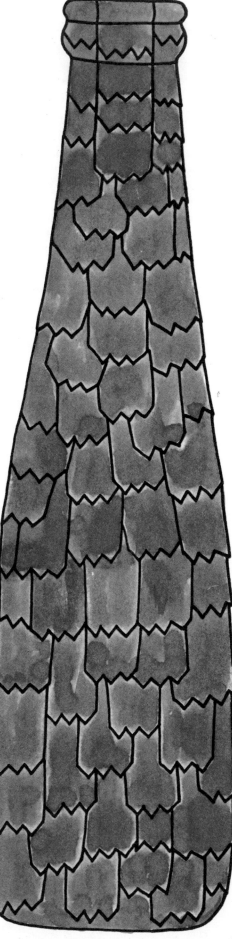

Baloo Drops In

Mowgli the Man-cub had no closer friend than Baloo the bear, with whom he spent many a care-free day. On this particular late afternoon, Baloo was lounging on his back in a cool pond, and Mowgli was perched on top of the bear's big stomach.

The sun was setting and a ray of light flickered through the trees, hitting a drowsy Baloo in the eye. He turned to one side to shield his eyes, forgetting Mowgli. Plop! The Man-cub landed in the pond.

"Sorry, Little Britches," Baloo chuckled. "Forgot you were up there."

"It's okay," Mowgli mumbled, reaching the edge of the pond and shaking beads of water out of his hair. "I'm tired of loafing, anyway. Let's go find Bagheera."

At that moment, Bagheera was far away watching some Men who had dug a deep pit in the middle of a jungle path and were covering it with branches. The black panther knew that the Men had set a trap, and he started off to warn the jungle folk.

Baloo and Mowgli, however, were blithely unaware of what Man had been doing in their jungle. As they strolled down a path, Baloo reached up and pulled two bananas off a branch and gave one to the Man-cub.

"Let's see if you can do this," Baloo challenged, peeling one banana and flipping the fresh fruit into the air. It landed neatly in his mouth. Mowgli giggled and tried the same trick, but he missed the banana and it hit his nose.

Baloo laughed. "You need more practice," he called as he lumbered heedlessly down the trail, looking up into the trees for more bananas. Mowgli was meandering along behind him a minute later when he heard a loud crash.

"Mowgli!" Baloo roared, shaking the jungle with his startled cry. Sure enough, the bear had fallen into the Man trap.

Bagheera heard the call and arrived on the scene. The branches covering the pit had given way under Baloo's weight. Wedged into the bottom of the pit was a helpless Baloo, lying on his back, his arms and legs pinned upward.

Bagheera's shiny black coat bristled with annoyance. "Oh, Baloo," he sighed. "I might have known I could count on you to blunder into this trap.''

Baloo couldn't move—he couldn't even wiggle, so tightly was he held, and he felt miserable. He looked up and saw Mowgli peering down at him. ''Oh, Bagheera!'' cried the Man-cub. ''What'll we do?''

''Whatever we do, it must be quick,'' replied Bagheera. ''We must free Baloo tonight. Man will be back tomorrow to see what he has captured. If he finds Baloo here . . . '' Bagheera's voice trailed off when he thought of what might happen.

''I'm hungry,'' wailed Baloo, who did not want to be both uncomfortable and hungry all night.

''This is no time to think of your stomach,'' scolded Bagheera. ''Keep quiet so we can think.''

Deep shadows fell in the jungle, and a full moon replaced the setting sun. Bagheera and Mowgli sat by the trap, silently pondering what to do.

''Could you lower me down by my feet so I could grab Baloo?'' Mowgli suggested. Bagheera looked down at the helpless bear and shook his head.

''He's too far down and too well stuck. We need some real strength,'' the panther muttered. Bagheera, his black shadow touching nearby trees, walked over to some vines. ''Mowgli, pull some of these down. We'll fasten them together and tie one end to a tree. Then we'll see if Baloo can pull himself out.''

The two friends lowered a length of vine into the pit and encouraged Baloo. But Bagheera's worst fear was realized when the vine broke in half under Baloo's gigantic weight.

As the wise old panther sat down again to ponder his next move, he heard a distant thundering noise. Then the marching beat caught Mowgli's attention. He looked at Bagheera. ''The elephant patrol!'' they gasped. Bagheera sprinted away and Mowgli followed.

''Hey, guys! Where are you going? Don't leave me here alone,'' yelled Baloo. But his friends had already left. The bear's forlorn groan floated up from the trap.

Bagheera and Mowgli came to the clearing where old Colonel Hathi was drilling his elephants. ''Halt!'' called Bagheera, muffling his

voice and using an old trick to stop the patrol. The elephants obediently halted, bumping into each other. A surprised Colonel Hathi looked around.

"Who said 'Halt!'?" he thundered, staring at his disordered platoon.

"I did," answered Bagheera, flowing out into the moonlit clearing. "I need your help. Baloo is stuck in a trap set by Man."

"Help? My help?" huffed Hathi. "Out of the question. We're on patrol."

"But, my dear Colonel," purred the panther, "only someone with great strength, such as yourself, can help."

"Besides," put in Mowgli, "you wouldn't want Man to succeed."

"Well, hrumph—in that case," replied Hathi, flattered by Bagheera's reference to his great strength, "we can't refuse. Forward, march!" And the elephant patrol followed the panther and the Man-cub out of the clearing.

Once at the trap, Colonel Hathi took charge. "Stand back, men," he bellowed. "This job requires my personal attention." And he stepped up to the pit and stretched out his trunk.

"Sorry, old chap, can't reach him," the Colonel snorted. He had placed his feet as close to the opening of the pit as he dared and stretched his

neck as far as he could. Baloo, stuck tightly at the bottom, tried mightily to reach Hathi's trunk, but it was no use.

Bagheera took a deep breath as the elephants looked on. "We have to think of something," he sighed. "Man will be here when the sun comes up."

Mowgli was sitting away from the group, looking glumly at the broken vine. Suddenly he brightened. "I've got it!" he exclaimed, and bounded away through the jungle, leaving a puzzled Bagheera staring after him.

Not far away, Mowgli found what he was looking for—the lair of Kaa, the python. Kaa was in the midst of hypnotizing a large insect for a late snack when he heard Mowgli calling him. He lowered his head down from the branch where he was coiled. "Here I am," Kaa hissed happily, and immediately tried to hypnotize the boy with his snaky stare.

"Ssso nice to sssee you," he whispered.

"C'mon Kaa, this is no time to hiss around," said Mowgli, tugging on the python's tail. Kaa lost his balance and toppled off the branch.

"We need your help," added the Man-cub. "Kaa?" But the great reptile was so dazed from his fall that he couldn't even refuse. Mowgli, interpreting the snake's silence to mean "yes," grabbed Kaa by the tail and proceeded to drag him back through the jungle to the pit where Baloo was trapped.

When Mowgli arrived back at the trap with the addled python, he explained his plan. Colonel Hathi stepped up to the edge of the pit again. This time he had Kaa's tail firmly gripped in his trunk.

"Just a moment," said Bagheera. "Kaa just might wake up before we're through with him. Just to be safe, Mowgli, take some leaves and a length of vine and blindfold him, so he won't be able to hypnotize anyone."

"Hey, Baggy-buddy!" Baloo's voice came bellowing out of the trap. "You'd better hurry. The sky's already turning pink!"

Colonel Hathi lowered the snake's length down to Baloo, who held onto Kaa with all his considerable might. The Colonel backed up slowly, step by step. Kaa felt his muscled body being pulled from both ends, but blindfolded as he was, he couldn't do anything about it. Hathi strained, Kaa

hissed, and Baloo wriggled. Suddenly, *pop*! Bear and snake came flying out of the trap.

Baloo picked up a dazed Kaa and patted him clumsily on the head. "Never thought I'd see you do a good deed, ol' slimy sides. But thanks a lot." And he removed the blindfold.

Kaa hissed a few times, but still couldn't focus his stare, so he creaked off into the undergrowth, muttering something about moving to another neighborhood.

The sun was up by now, and it was time for the animals to leave the empty trap for Man to find. Baloo took hold of Mowgli's hand and they followed Bagheera into the jungle.

"Thanks to you, too, Little Britches," said Baloo. "I thought I was a goner."

"Well," huffed Bagheera, "I hope you've learned your lesson."

"Sure, Baggy-buddy," replied the bear. "The next time I eat a banana, I'll watch out for the pits!"

BEACH PATTERNS

Waves rush to meet the shore, then retreat to the ocean deep. Each wave leaves its own pattern in the sand. It may last only until the next wave comes. One pattern is washed away, another takes its place.

In some places, the waves carry sands and other material from the ocean bottom up onto the beach. In other places or at other times, the waves carry sands away from the beaches. As a result, beaches are always changing. Some get wider, others get narrower. Some are decorated with shells and bits of coral, others have pebbles worn smooth by tumbling waters.

The wind also plays an important role in creating beach patterns. It picks up light grains of sand, leaving behind the heavier ones, which may be differently colored. The wind may carry the grains far away, even depositing them on other shores.

Wind and water often work together. In winter, when temperatures drop below freezing, water and sand may form solid blocks—rather like what would form if you filled an ice-cube tray with very wet sand. The wind attacks the blocks of sand, sculpting out soft spots, rounding edges, widening cracks.

If you walk along a beach, you can help the waves create interesting beach patterns. Place a shell or pebble in the sand. Watch what happens as the water flows over it and then retreats. Your object diverts the return flow of water, so that a pattern of diverging lines forms in the sand.

Next, look for the two most common patterns left by the water: ripples and swash marks. Ripples look like the surface of a piece of corrugated cardboard. In between the crests of the ridges are shallow depres-

This pattern was made by wind and waves, which removed the white sand faster than the heavier red sand.

This pattern was formed over many years by winds that carried sand from Africa to the Canary Islands.

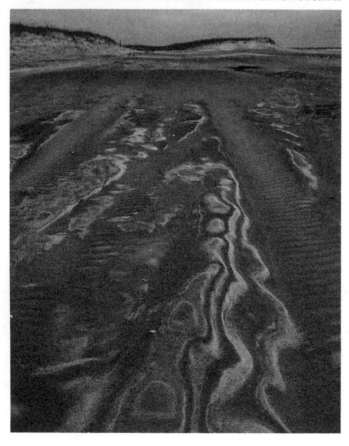

sions. Often, the depressions glisten in the sunlight. This is due to tiny pieces of the mineral mica, which were left behind by the retreating waves.

Swash marks indicate the highest spot on the beach reached by waves. As a wave rushes up the beach, it carries sand, bits of plants, shells, and other material. When the wave reaches its highest point, it deposits this sediment, then recedes. The line formed by the sediment—the swash mark—is often concave. As the tide goes out, each wave moves a shorter distance up the beach than the previous wave. Thus it is that a pattern of concave lines is formed along a flat sandy beach.

All these different patterns can be photographed. Enlarged and mounted, the photographs make beautiful works of art that can be displayed in your home or given as gifts to friends. So the next time you walk along a beach, take along a camera and look for the patterns.

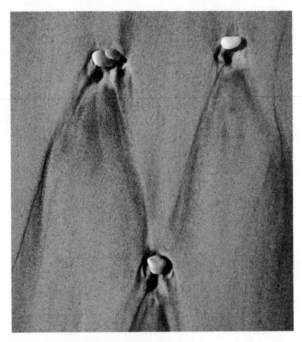

Retreating waves created this pattern of diverging lines in the sand around these pebbles.

In many places, waves deposit lovely shells and bits of coral on the beach. Each one of these remains of living things has its own interesting pattern.

THE BEES ARE COMING

One of the common sounds of summer is the hum of honeybees as they flit about the garden. These gentle insects have always been thought of as nature's helpers. They carry pollen from bloom to bloom, making the flowers develop into fruit. Bees make honey, too—that delicious natural food. Of course we know that bees can sting, but they usually do that only when disturbed. And a person will usually suffer stings from only a bee or two.

All this is true of the type of honeybee living in North America and Europe. These bees are called European bees. But in South America another type of honeybee, originally from Africa, is making many people nervous. It is not gentle. In fact, its nickname has become "the killer bee." And this bee is moving toward North America.

But let's take a closer look at this killer bee and the stories that have sprung up about it.

▶ THE AFRICAN BEE

We'll begin in Africa, where William Lyon, a bee specialist, had a frightening encounter with the killer bees. The young American was working in the eastern African country of Kenya several years ago when a Kenyan woman came to him for help. She owned a house that she wanted to rent out, but could not do so because a large colony of African honeybees had moved into one of the walls. No one, of course, wanted to live under the same roof with a great many bees. Would Lyon help her get rid of them?

Lyon agreed to help her and went, with an assistant, to her house. He knew that this particular kind of bee could mean trouble. But his assistant, who was less familiar with the bees, abruptly yanked a board off the side of the house. Thousands of bees sprang from their nest and began stinging everyone and everything in sight.

The villagers fled in all directions. But the bees continued to chase them, stinging men, women, children, and animals. The bees even entered other village huts and attacked the people they found there. No one was safe, not even Lyon and his helper in their beekeeper suits. These special suits have snug-fitting cuffs around the ankles and wrists to prevent bees from getting inside, and there is a bonnet with a veil to protect the face and neck. Beekeepers usually wear these suits whenever they handle bees. But the suits didn't do much for Lyon and his assistant. The bees were able to wriggle under the edges of the veils.

It was a horrible experience. But Lyon finally brought the bees under control by going back to his laboratory, picking up backpacks of insecticide, returning to the village, and spraying them.

It is incidents like this that have earned this little honeybee the name of "killer bee." Some writers have even gone so far as to declare that the bees have a natural hatred for human beings because humans have been raiding the insects' hives and taking their honey for thousands of years.

Scientists say that explanations like this are nonsense. People have always taken the honey from all kinds of honeybees—why should the African kind be the only one to have this intense hatred?

The more likely reason for the African bee's alarming fierceness is to be found in its genes, the tiny biochemical units of heredity we all carry.

The African bee's genes probably make it a tough little fighter. And because it is a tough little fighter, it has been able to defend itself and its hive against other creatures that would prey upon it—creatures like army ants, armadillos, wasps, and, of course, people. By defending itself, the bee has survived.

The African bee is also very sensitive to disturbances of any kind, and it responds with great vigor. When a human acts this way, we say that the person has a "quick temper" or a "short fuse."

Scientists are pretty sure that when any bee stings something, it releases into the air a biochemical substance called a *pheromone*. Pheromones, which have a chemical property that bees recognize, are, in effect, messages. Insects use them to communicate with one another. And so when the first few bees in a hive are disturbed and attack the offending party—whether it be a cow, a column of ants, or a human—their stinging sends out alarm calls to the other bees in the hive. The alarms summon the other bees to the defense of the hive.

When an African hive is disturbed, large numbers of bees give chase. So the alarm process snowballs: more bees mean more stings. More stings mean the release of more pheromones. More pheromones mean more bees called into action. More bees, more stings. And so on.

"Fool around with ordinary honeybees," said one specialist, "and you may get ten or fifteen stings as you escape. But fool around with these African bees, and you may get several hundred stings before you can finally get away from them."

It is the large amount of venom that hundreds of bees inject into a victim that makes them such a hazard to other creatures. The venom itself is basically no different from that of other types of honeybees.

▶THE AFRICAN BEE REACHES SOUTH AMERICA

Back in 1956, government scientists in Brazil decided to import some African bees.

The Brazilians knew that the African bee was a fierce insect, but they also knew that it was a hard worker and an excellent producer of top-quality honey.

The plan was to crossbreed the African bees with the gentle European bees kept by Brazilian beekeepers and farmers. The scientists hoped the crossbreeding would produce a bee that would be easy to handle but would also fly far and wide in search of food. This searching, known as foraging, is very important in agriculture because the bees carry pollen for different fruit crops as they fly from blossom to blossom. This process, called pollination, enables plants to bear fruit.

But the Brazilians never got the chance to carry out their plan. A beekeeper accidentally released most of the queen bees into the wild. And their descendants (called Africanized bees) have been spreading across South America ever since. Today the bee can be found throughout Brazil, Uruguay, Argentina, Venezuela, and parts of Colombia and French Guiana. And it is these bees that are heading for North America.

What has happened as the bees have spread out over wider and wider areas? Have they caused widespread death and de-

An Africanized bee collects water from water plants. The water will be brought back to the hive, where it will cool the colony by evaporation.

struction? Apparently not. There have been a number of reported cases of humans dying as a result of massive stinging by colonies of Africanized bees, but only one or two are considered to be true stories.

Several groups of American bee experts have visited South America in the past few years to get a firsthand look at the Africanized bee. They have found out some interesting things.

First of all, not all Africanized bees are equally vicious. Although all these bees (which look nearly the same as the European honeybees most people are familiar with) must be treated carefully, it does seem that only some of them are likely to go on stinging rampages. This difference between one group and another tells scientists that the reason for the bees' behavior must be in their genes.

Secondly, experiences with the bee in southern Brazil, Uruguay, and Argentina show that its ferocity can be brought under control. In those regions, there were large populations of gentle European honeybees. The Africanized bees that invaded those countries mated with the resident bees. The offspring of these matings were very much like what the Brazilian scientists had had in mind when they imported African bees: hard-working, productive honeybees.

Whenever beekeepers or farmers in those southern areas found a colony of bees whose fierceness had not been lessened by crossbreeding with more gentle local bees, they either removed the queen bee from the hive and destroyed her (since only the queen lays eggs) or destroyed the entire colony.

There are well-established bee populations in Costa Rica and other parts of Central America and in Mexico, and crossbreeding with these should help soften the Africanized bee's fierce nature. Vicious colonies or vicious queens will have to be spotted and destroyed.

One thing is clear, say the experts: the bee will never be brought under control by insecticides. Any poison that kills bad bees will also kill good bees. But by carefully planned breeding programs and by the destruction of ferocious individual bees, the Africanized bee may become a welcome guest to North America when it arrives here—probably sometime in the early 1990's.

GEORGE ALEXANDER
Science Writer
The Los Angeles Times

Pompeii, as it stands today.

ONE DAY IN POMPEII

It was August 24, in the year A.D. 79. The place was Pompeii—a Roman city located in Italy, south of Naples. About 20,000 people lived there.

As the sun rose in the early morning, it brought the promise of a beautiful day. People awoke and got up. They saw the sun and were happy. Soon the people were busy working. Pompeii had many restaurants, wine shops, bakeries, and stores. There were shops where wool fabrics were woven and factories where pottery and iron tools were made. There were olive groves and vineyards in the city's outskirts.

In the homes, women gave orders to their slaves. Perhaps they went outside into their gardens. And as they picked flowers, perhaps they looked up at nearby Mount Vesuvius. "How beautiful the mountain looks," they may have thought. "How peaceful is the day."

BOOM! Around midday the peace was shattered by a huge noise. It sounded like thunder, and the ground shook. In the homes, all kinds of objects tumbled from shelves.

When people looked up at Vesuvius, they saw the most amazing sight. It had blown its top! Never before in recorded history had Mount Vesuvius done this. Flames and rocks were shooting from the mountain, and liquid rock (lava) poured out. Clouds of ash and poisonous smoke formed.

Soon the day turned as dark as night. Rocks and ash began falling on Pompeii. The fiery red lava ran down the mountainside toward the town. The people were confused and didn't know what to do. Some

Archeologists uncovered this magnificent dining room in a town near Pompeii.

This wall portrait of a man and his wife was found in a home next to a Pompeii bakery.

Many beautiful treasures that were found in Pompeii toured the United States in 1978. Included were this wall painting of a leopard (*above*); this silver hand mirror (*left*); and these emerald-and-gold earrings (*below*).

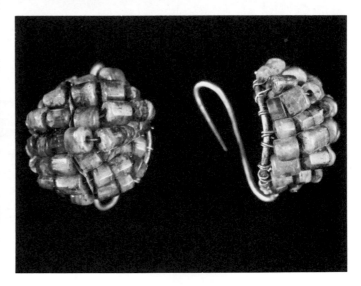

gathered in the town's big exercise ground, near the arena. Others sought safety in their homes. They closed the shutters and doors and waited for the eruption to end. A few of the richer families loaded their belongings onto donkeys and began to leave town. Chances are, they didn't escape. Like those who stayed behind, they were probably trapped by the flowing lava or choked to death by the poisonous gases.

In less than three days, Mount Vesuvius was calm again. The eruption was over. All was very quiet in Pompeii. It was quiet because the city had disappeared—buried beneath 20 feet (6 meters) of lava and ash. And all its inhabitants were dead and buried, too.

As far as we know, no one from Pompeii escaped and lived to write about this terrible event. But we have an account of the eruption written by a young Roman named Pliny. He was staying in a seaside town west of Mount Vesuvius. Wrote Pliny:

"On August 24, in the early afternoon, my mother drew attention to a cloud of unusual size and appearance ... best expressed as being like an umbrella pine, for it rose to a great height on a sort of trunk and

then split off into branches . . . on Mount Vesuvius broad sheets of fire and leaping flames blazed at several points."

The buildings in the seaside town were shaking and, the next day, Pliny and his mother left the town. Together with many other people, they traveled along a road that led away from the mountain. "Ashes were already falling, not yet very thickly," wrote Pliny. "I looked around: A dense black cloud was coming up behind us, spreading over the earth like a flood.

"[Soon] darkness fell, not the dark of a moonless or cloudy night, but as if the lamp had been put out in a closed room. You could hear the shrieks of the women, the wailing of infants, and the shouting of men."

Time passed and, eventually, "the darkness thinned and dispersed like smoke or cloud . . . the sun actually shone out, but yellowish, as it is during an eclipse. We were terrified to see everything changed, buried deep in ashes like snowdrifts."

Several towns were permanently buried by the eruption. But the thick layer of lava and ash preserved the objects it covered. It kept them from rotting or rusting. It saved them from being stolen by robbers.

For almost 1,700 years, Pompeii remained buried—and forgotten. The city was discovered in the 1730's, and in 1748 people began excavating. This work continues even now. There are still parts of the city and its suburbs to be uncovered.

But archeologists (scientists who study the remains of past human activities and civilizations) have uncovered large areas of the city. Today tourists can walk along roads where chariots raced. They can enter temples where the people of Pompeii worshipped. They can sit in theaters where Greek comedies were performed.

The archeologists also found many beautiful objects that were used in the buildings of Pompeii. Some of these are displayed at Pompeii. Others are kept in museums elsewhere, particularly in Naples. And in 1978, and exhibit of 300 of the most interesting treasures began a tour of the United States. The exhibit opened in Boston, went to Chicago and Dallas, and will end in New York in 1979.

The exhibit includes models of Pompeii and of one of the city's houses. There are sculptures, mosaics, and wall paintings. There are toys, tools, and gold jewelry. But perhaps the objects that one remembers longest are two plaster casts. As they uncovered Pompeii, archeologists found impressions of bodies in the ash. They made casts of these. One is of a sleeping dog. The other is of a young woman. She holds her dress up over her face, trying to keep from breathing the poisonous air. But her efforts were in vain. Like the bakers and woolmakers, the wine merchants and chariot riders, she died on that terrible August day 1,900 years ago.

ADOPT AN ANIMAL

"Please Don't Feed the Animals."

You see that disappointing sign in just about every zoo you go to. If you bring a pocketful of peanuts for the elephant, you usually have to eat them yourself.

But what's this? A new sign! And this one says, "Please *Do* Feed the Animals."

That's right. Many zoos are beginning to ask people to feed their animals. But instead of asking you to reach into your pocket for peanuts, the zoos would rather you reached in for money.

Like everyone else, zoos have been faced with budget problems. The cost of animal food, in particular, has gone way up. So some zoos have come up with a solution to the problem: ask people to "adopt" an animal. An animal lover could choose his or her favorite animal, pay its food bills for the year, and become the animal's "foster parent." As a foster parent, you may not take "your" animal out for a stroll, but you do receive the joy of helping the animal.

The first zoo to try the "adopt-an-animal" program was the Columbus, Ohio, zoo. Other zoos, such as the Brookfield Zoo near Chicago, also have successful programs. Often, an individual person or a family will adopt an animal. Sometimes a class in a school—or the whole school—will raise the money to adopt an animal.

What does it cost to adopt a zoo animal? That depends on the animal. It takes only $10 to feed an Australian flying squirrel for one year. But it takes $2,000 to buy enough fish for a dolphin's yearly fill. Between these two extremes you would pay $25 for a hedgehog and $50 for a medium-size snake. A llama will chomp down $100 worth of grain and grasses, and a leopard will lick its chops over $400 worth of meat. A tiger may cost you $800, a gorilla about $1,000, and a hippopotamus about $1,500.

So if you'd like to become a "zoo parent," please do feed the animals—but not with popcorn and peanuts. Make it cash instead!

SPOON PEOPLE

This pretty lady was once a plain wooden spoon. Now she hangs on a wall, holding flowers in her pocket. You can make this spoon lady, or any other spoon person you can think of.

What to Use:

a wooden cooking spoon
yarn—about 1 yard (1 meter), of a color to be used for hair
fabric—a 12-inch (30-centimeter) square
felt—small scraps, of colors to be used for lips and eyes
glue, scissors, lace or other decoration

What to Do:

1. Cut a square piece of fabric for the dress. Each side of the square should be as long as the handle of the spoon.

2. Cut a small piece of fabric for the pocket. You can use a contrasting fabric if you wish.

3. Hem the dress on the bottom, and the pocket on all four sides. Sew your decoration onto the dress. Then sew the pocket onto the front of the dress.

4. Assemble all your materials on a clean sheet of newspaper. The "face" of the spoon is the round, convex side.

5. Make a loop with which to hang the spoon: Cut a 6-inch (15-centimeter) piece of yarn. Make a double loop. Glue the loose ends of the loop onto the top back of the spoon. The loop should clear the top of the spoon by about an inch (2.5 centimeters).

6. Cut 10 strands of yarn for the hair. Try arranging the strands in different ways. You may want to cut a few extra short pieces for bangs. When you have a nice arrangement, glue the yarn onto the spoon. The top ends should be glued over the back of the spoon.

7. Cut two eyes and a mouth from the felt. Then glue these onto the face.

8. Glue the dress onto the handle of the spoon. First, glue the center top of the dress onto the front neck of the spoon handle. When this is dry, bring the top edges of the dress around the back of the handle and glue down. Do this at an angle, so that the dress has a nice flared look.

9. The pocket in the spoon person's dress can be used for many things: dried flowers, a box of matches, small emery boards, toothpicks, pencils.

THE WEALTH OF THE ANTARCTIC

A vast, frozen continent lies at the southernmost reaches of the world. Its name is Antarctica, and it is the coldest place on Earth. Almost all of Antarctica's more than 5,000,000 square miles (12,950,000 square kilometers) are covered with ice. A temperature of −127°F (−88°C) has been recorded at the South Pole.

Yet out of this frozen world may come the solution to one of the world's most serious problems: food shortages and starvation. This is because the seas around Antarctica are rich with fish. The question is, can the nations of the world agree on how to harvest the Antarctic's wonderful wealth?

▶JOURNEYS TO THE BOTTOM OF THE WORLD

Explorers were attracted to the Antarctic long before anyone suspected that its seas might solve the world's food problems. The English sea captain James Cook led two ships in a voyage toward the South Pole in the 1770's. He did not land on Antarctica, but his ships certainly entered the iceberg-filled Antarctic seas. An American sea captain, John Davis, is believed to have been the first to land on Antarctica, in 1821.

By the early part of the 20th century, many countries had sent explorers, including the United States, Russia, Britain, France, Australia, and Norway. And in 1911, the Norwegian Roald Amundsen became the first to reach the South Pole, the very "bottom of the world."

▶CO-OPERATION OR CONFLICT?

Throughout the 20th century, scientific research and further exploration have gone on in the Antarctic. The research has been conducted mostly by five nations: Belgium, Japan, South Africa, the United States, and the Soviet Union.

To some extent, the nations that have bases on Antarctica have co-operated with each other. During the International Geophysical Year (1957–58), twelve nations set up scientific research bases in the Antarctic.

There have, however, been disputes between some nations as to who should control portions of the Antarctic. Seven nations—Argentina, Australia, Britain, Chile, France, New Zealand, and Norway—have all claimed parts of the Antarctic continent as their own. And some of these nations are claiming the same land. This has led to problems. Who owns Antarctica? Should anyone? Or does the continent at the bottom of the world belong to everyone?

The Antarctic Treaty of 1959 tried to deal with some of these problems. This treaty, signed by the five researching nations and the seven land-claiming nations, stated that no land claim may be added to or subtracted from. The treaty also provided for co-operation between the nations. And it stated that the Antarctic regions would be open to explorers and researchers from all nations.

▶NATURAL RESOURCES

In the early 1960's, the world became aware of the huge fishing resources of the Antarctic seas. In particular, a shrimplike crustacean (shellfish) called krill abounds in those chilly southern waters. There is so much krill, in fact, that food scientists hope that krill may one day provide most of the world's protein.

There are other fish as well. Japanese and Soviet fishing boats have caught hundreds of thousands of tons of cod in recent years. Some experts believe that the Antarctic waters may soon produce 100,000,000 tons of fish a year. That amount would equal the yearly catch in the whole rest of the world!

But now the question of international co-operation comes up again. The "hungry" nations of the world will want, and need, a fair share of this huge protein supply. Yet it is the wealthier nations that are better able to harvest all that fish. If the world's nations cannot agree on Antarctic land claims, will they be able to agree on the distribution of fishing rights?

And there is another problem, one that is connected with krill fishing. This is the problem of the Antarctic environment. Many Antarctic animals—such as whales, penguins, seals, squid, and fish—depend upon krill for their food. If too much krill is caught for humans, will these other creatures die out?

Krill may one day provide most of the world's protein.

In addition to the fish supply, there are also valuable minerals and oil in the Antarctic. Only the highly industrialized countries are capable of extracting these riches from the earth. Again, the question—will the world's poorer nations be kept from sharing this Antarctic wealth?

▶THE CANBERRA CONFERENCE

In an attempt to answer some of these questions, a thirteen-nation conference was held in Canberra, Australia, in early 1978. The twelve signers of the 1959 treaty were joined by Poland.

The Canberra Conference concentrated mainly on the harvesting of the protein-rich krill. There were many disagreements among the nations. But they did agree to create a commission that would control krill fishing in the Antarctic waters. The commission would have the power to set up fishing quotas. Experts would examine the effect of krill fishing on the Antarctic environment.

The conference marked an important step toward international co-operation. However, there is still much to be worked out and more meetings were scheduled. And the old problem of the "ownership" of the Antarctic will not go away. It is especially hoped that the later conferences will not dissolve into an argument over a question that is as old as the human race: whose is it—yours, mine, or ours?

DANIEL J. DOMOFF
Consulting Editor
Educational Developmental Laboratories

FRISBEE-CATCHING CANINES

The Frisbee whirls through the air. A player named Dink springs into action. He catches the disc before his feet hit the ground. What accuracy! What a dog!

Dink is a lucky dog, too. Jim Strickler saw him in a Pittsburgh dog pound and took him home as a pet. His new owner also taught Dink to catch a Frisbee.

Dink learned to run after the flying disc, leap into the air to grab it with his teeth, and then bring the Frisbee back to his master. He became so good at catching and fetching Frisbees that Jim entered him in a few contests. And Dink kept winning.

Then, after only eighteen months of training, Dink made the finals of the 1978 World K-9 Frisbee Championship. This canine contest was held in the Rose Bowl stadium in Pasadena, California, as part of the fifth annual World Frisbee Championships.

Three other dogs also reached the finals, which were seen by 50,000 people. Ashley Whippet, who had been the world champ for three straight years, ended up in second place. Toke came in third; and Ivey Lee, fourth. Dink placed first — becoming the world's greatest Frisbee-catching canine. Dink was awarded a $1,000 savings bond and all the dog food he could eat for one year.

No one knows Dink's age or breed, but his owner/trainer thinks one of the dog's parents must have been a Labrador retriever. "Dink just loves to chase Frisbees and bring them back to me," says Jim. The day Dink won the championship, his happy owner gave him a big steak for dinner!

Any dog can compete for Dink's title as the world champ. Preliminary catch-and-fetch tournaments, sponsored by park and recreation departments, are held during the summer in more than 500 cities across the United States. Nine regional winners are chosen, and they compete for the honor of performing at the world Frisbee finals in the Rose Bowl.

In the all-important finals, the dogs perform one at a time and are awarded points by the judges. During two minutes of catch-and-fetch competition, a point is given each time a dog catches a Frisbee thrown by its master at least 45 feet (13.7 meters). If a catch is made with all four paws off the ground, the dog gets an extra point. The dogs are also allowed three minutes of freestyle performance. They are judged on their style and agility in catching and returning the plastic discs.

A little booklet has been written about how to teach your dog to catch a flying Frisbee. To receive a free copy of this booklet, write to:

> Gaines Dog Research Center
> 250 North Street
> White Plains, New York 10625

For information about local K-9 catch-and-fetch contests, write to:

> Lander and Associates
> 5430 Van Nuys Boulevard
> Van Nuys, California 91401

MICHELE AND TOM GRIMM
Authors, *What Is a Seal?*

Former world champion, Ashley Whippet.

This catch made with four paws in the air earned Dink an extra point.

INDEX

ILLUSTRATION CREDITS
AND ACKNOWLEDGMENTS

18–Bob Campbell—Bruce
19 Coleman
20–Jan Braunle
21
23 Thomas D. W. Friedmann
—Photo Researchers
24 ©James Pollock—National
Audubon Society/Photo Researchers
25 John Wheatley
27 United States–China
People's Friendship Association and Environmental
Communications
28–Robert R. McElroy—
29 Newsweek
31 Jenny Tesar
32–Courtesy of Scholastic Photography Awards, conducted
33 tography Awards, conducted
by Scholastic Magazines,
Inc., and sponsored by
Eastman Kodak Company
38 Harry Engels
39 Peter D. Capen; C.A. Morgan
40 Harry Engels; Charlie
Ott—National Audubon
Society/Photo Researchers;
Roman Vishniac
41 Charlie Ott—National Audubon Society/Photo Researchers; Larry West
42 Ann Hagen Griffiths—DPI
44 Musée d'Art et d'Histoire,
Neuchâtel, Suisse
45 UPI

46 Queen's Devices, Inc.
47 Westinghouse Science Talent Search
48 Sipa Press/Black Star
49 Mike Norcia—Photoreporters
50 Sipa Press/Black Star
52 Mike Wells
54 BBC Copyright Photographs
55 Mike Wells
56–Adapted from Pocket Cal-
57 culator Fun & Games by
Ross and Pat Olney. Text
©1977 by Ross R. Olney. By
permission of Franklin
Watts, Inc.
62–Courtesy The American
63 Museum of Natural History
65 Courtesy Smithsonian Institution
66–Presented by Pentel of
67 America, Ltd.
68 Run For Life/Connecticut
Mutual Life Insurance Co.
via Authenticated News
International
71 Focus On Sports
72 William C. Blizzard
74 William C. Blizzard;
William C. Blizzard; Dolly
Sherwood
75 Courtesy State of West Virginia, Department of Culture
and History
82–Peter D. Capen
83

84–Courtesy Binney & Smith
87
88 John G. Ross—Photo Researchers
89 British Crown Copyright.
With the permission of the
Controller of Her Britannic
Majesty's Stationery Office
91 British Crown Copyright
92 Michael Putland—Retna
93 Jenny Tesar
94 Bettmann Archive
98–Jonathan Atkin
101
103 Judith Hoffman Corwin
108–Manny Rodriguez
109
110 Dr. Norman E. Gary
113 Dr. Norman E. Gary
114 Lobl—Shostal
115–Courtesy Xerox Corporation
116
119 Jan Braunle
121 Animals Animals/©Oxford
Scientific Films
123 Tom & Michele Grimm